Apollo 11 Photo

A 50ᵗʰ Anniversary Celebration

Steven Chabotte

ISBN: 1719008965
ISBN-13: 978-1719008969

CONTENTS

1 THE MISSION AND ITS OBJECTIVES

Mission Objective

The primary objective of Apollo 11 was to complete a national goal set by President John F. Kennedy on May 25, 1961: perform a crewed lunar landing and return to Earth.

Additional flight objectives included scientific exploration by the lunar module, or LM, crew; deployment of a television camera to transmit signals to Earth; and deployment of a solar wind composition experiment, seismic experiment package and a Laser Ranging Retroreflector. During the exploration, the two astronauts were to gather samples of lunar-surface materials for return to Earth. They also were to extensively photograph the lunar terrain, the deployed scientific equipment, the LM spacecraft, and each other, both with still and motion picture cameras. This was to be the last Apollo mission to fly a "free-return" trajectory, which would enable a return to Earth with no engine firing, providing a ready abort of the mission at any time prior to lunar orbit insertion.

Mission Highlights

Apollo 11 launched from Cape Kennedy on July 16, 1969, carrying Commander Neil Armstrong, Command Module Pilot Michael Collins and Lunar Module Pilot Edwin "Buzz" Aldrin into an initial Earth-orbit of 114 by 116 miles. An estimated 530 million people watched Armstrong's televised image and heard his voice describe the event as he took "...one small step for a man, one giant leap for mankind" on July 20, 1969.

Two hours, 44 minutes and one-and-a-half revolutions after launch, the S-IVB stage reignited for a second burn of five minutes, 48 seconds, placing Apollo 11 into a translunar orbit. The command and service module, or CSM, Columbia separated from the stage, which included the spacecraft-lunar module adapter, or SLA, containing the lunar module, or LM, Eagle. After transposition and jettisoning of the SLA panels on the S-IVB stage, the CSM docked with the LM. The S-IVB stage separated and injected into heliocentric orbit four hours, 40 minutes into the flight.

The first color TV transmission to Earth from Apollo 11 occurred during the translunar coast of the CSM/LM. Later, on July 17, a three-second burn of the SPS was made to perform the second of four scheduled midcourse corrections programmed for the flight. The launch had been so successful that the other three were not needed.

On July 18, Armstrong and Aldrin put on their spacesuits and climbed through the docking tunnel from Columbia to Eagle to check out the LM, and to make the second TV transmission.

On July 19, after Apollo 11 had flown behind the moon out of contact with Earth, came the first lunar orbit insertion maneuver. At about 75 hours, 50 minutes into the flight, a retrograde firing of the SPS for 357.5 seconds placed the spacecraft into an initial, elliptical-lunar orbit of 69 by 190 miles. Later, a second burn of the SPS for 17 seconds placed the docked vehicles into a lunar orbit of 62 by 70.5 miles, which was calculated to change the orbit of the CSM piloted by Collins. The change happened because of lunar-gravity perturbations to the nominal 69 miles required for subsequent LM rendezvous and docking after completion of the lunar landing. Before this second SPS firing, another TV transmission was made, this time from the surface of the moon.

On July 20, Armstrong and Aldrin entered the LM again, made a final check, and at 100 hours, 12 minutes into the flight, the Eagle undocked and separated from Columbia for visual inspection. At 101 hours, 36 minutes, when the LM was behind the moon on its 13th orbit, the LM descent engine fired for 30 seconds to provide retrograde thrust and commence descent orbit insertion, changing to an orbit of 9 by 67 miles, on a trajectory that was virtually identical to that flown by Apollo 10. At 102 hours, 33 minutes, after Columbia and Eagle had reappeared from behind the moon and when the LM was about 300 miles uprange, powered descent initiation was performed with the descent engine firing for 756.3 seconds. After eight minutes, the LM was at "high gate" about 26,000 feet above the surface and about five miles from the landing site.

The descent engine continued to provide braking thrust until about 102 hours, 45 minutes into the mission. Partially piloted manually by Armstrong, the Eagle landed in the Sea of Tranquility in Site 2 at 0 degrees, 41 minutes, 15 seconds north latitude and 23 degrees, 26 minutes east longitude. This was about four miles downrange from the predicted touchdown point and occurred almost one-and-a-half minutes earlier than scheduled. It included a powered descent that ran a mere nominal 40 seconds longer than preflight planning due to translation maneuvers to avoid a crater during the final phase of landing. Attached to the descent stage was a commemorative plaque signed by President Richard M. Nixon and the three astronauts.

The flight plan called for the first EVA to begin after a four-hour rest period, but it was advanced to begin as soon as possible. Nonetheless, it was almost four hours later that Armstrong emerged from the Eagle and deployed the TV camera for the transmission of the event to Earth. At about 109 hours, 42 minutes after launch, Armstrong stepped onto the moon. About 20 minutes later, Aldrin followed him. The camera was then positioned on a tripod about 30 feet from the LM. Half an hour later, President Nixon spoke by telephone link with the astronauts.

Commemorative medallions bearing the names of the three Apollo 1 astronauts who lost their lives in a launch pad fire, and two cosmonauts who also died in accidents, were left on the moon's surface. A one-

and-a-half inch silicon disk, containing micro miniaturized goodwill messages from 73 countries, and the names of congressional and NASA leaders, also stayed behind.

During the EVA, in which they both ranged up to 300 feet from the Eagle, Aldrin deployed the Early Apollo Scientific Experiments Package, or EASEP, experiments, and Armstrong and Aldrin gathered and verbally reported on the lunar surface samples. After Aldrin had spent one hour, 33 minutes on the surface, he re-entered the LM, followed 41 minutes later by Armstrong. The entire EVA phase lasted more than two-and-a-half hours, ending at 111 hours, 39 minutes into the mission.

Armstrong and Aldrin spent 21 hours, 36 minutes on the moon's surface. After a rest period that included seven hours of sleep, the ascent stage engine fired at 124 hours, 22 minutes. It was shut down 435 seconds later when the Eagle reached an initial orbit of 11 by 55 miles above the moon, and when Columbia was on its 25th revolution. As the ascent stage reached apolune at 125 hours, 19 minutes, the reaction control system, or RCS, fired so as to nearly circularize the Eagle orbit at about 56 miles, some 13 miles below and slightly behind Columbia. Subsequent firings of the LM RCS changed the orbit to 57 by 72 miles. Docking with Columbia occurred on the CSM's 27th revolution at 128 hours, three minutes into the mission. Armstrong and Aldrin returned to the CSM with Collins. Four hours later, the LM jettisoned and remained in lunar orbit.

Trans-Earth injection of the CSM began July 21 as the SPS fired for two-and-a-half minutes when Columbia was behind the moon in its 59th hour of lunar orbit. Following this, the astronauts slept for about 10 hours. An 11.2 second firing of the SPS accomplished the only midcourse correction required on the return flight. The correction was made July 22 at about 150 hours, 30 minutes into the mission. Two more television transmissions were made during the trans-Earth coast.

Re-entry procedures were initiated July 24, 44 hours after leaving lunar orbit. The SM separated from the CM, which was re-oriented to a heat-shield-forward position. Parachute deployment occurred at 195 hours, 13 minutes. After a flight of 195 hours, 18 minutes, 35 seconds - about 36 minutes longer than planned - Apollo 11 splashed down in the Pacific Ocean, 13 miles from the recovery ship USS Hornet. Because of bad weather in the target area, the landing point was changed by about 250 miles. Apollo 11 landed 13 degrees, 19 minutes north latitude and 169 degrees, nine minutes west longitude July 24, 1969.

Crew
Neil Armstrong, Commander
Edwin E. Aldrin Jr., Lunar Module Pilot
Michael Collins, Command Module Pilot

Backup Crew
James A. Lovell, Commander
Fred W. Haise Jr., Lunar Module Pilot
William A. Anders, Command Module Pilot

Payload
Columbia (CSM-107)
Eagle (LM-5)

Prelaunch Milestones
11/21/68 - LM-5 integrated systems test
12/6/68 - CSM-107 integrated systems test
12/13/68 - LM-5 acceptance test
1/8/69 - LM-5 ascent stage delivered to Kennedy
1/12/69 - LM-5 descent stage delivered to Kennedy
1/18/69 - S-IVB ondock at Kennedy
1/23/69 - CSM ondock at Kennedy
1/29/69 - command and service module mated
2/6/69 - S-II ondock at Kennedy
2/20/69 - S-IC ondock at Kennedy
2/17/69 - combined CSM-107 systems tests
2/27/69 - S-IU ondock at Kennedy
3/24/69 - CSM-107 altitude testing
4/14/69 - rollover of CSM from the Operations and Checkout Building to the Vehicle Assembly Building
4/22/69 - integrated systems test
5/5/69 - CSM electrical mate to Saturn V
5/20/69 - rollout to Launch Pad 39A
6/1/69 - flight readiness test
6/26/69 - Countdown Demonstration Test

Launch
July 16, 1969; 9:32 a.m. EDT
Launch Pad 39A
Saturn-V AS-506
High Bay 1
Mobile Launcher Platform-1
Firing Room 1

Orbit
Altitude: 118.65 miles
Inclination: 32.521 degrees
Orbits: 30 revolutions
Duration: eight days, three hours, 18 min, 35 seconds
Distance: 953,054 miles
Lunar Location: Sea of Tranquility
Lunar Coordinates: .71 degrees north, 23.63 degrees east

Landing

July 24, 1969; 12:50 p.m. EDT
Pacific Ocean
Recovery Ship: USS Hornet

2 MEET THE CREW

The National Aeronautics and Space Administration (NASA) has named these three astronauts as the prime crew of the Apollo 11 lunar landing mission. Left to right, are Neil A. Armstrong, commander; Michael Collins, command module pilot; and Edwin E. Aldrin Jr., lunar module pilot.

Edwin E. "Buzz" Aldrin

Edwin E. Aldrin, Jr. (1930-) was born in Montclair, New Jersey, on 20 January 1930. He attended the U.S. Military Academy at West Point, entered the United States Air Force, and received pilot training in 1951. Aldrin flew sixty-six combat missions in F-86s in Korea, destroying two MIG-15 aircraft. Known to all as by his nickname, "Buzz," Aldrin was also one of the most important figures in the accomplishment of Project Apollo in successfully landing an American on the Moon in 1960s.

Aldrin became an astronaut during the selection of the third group by NASA in October 1963. On 11 November 1966 he orbited aboard the Gemini XII spacecraft, a 4-day 59-revolution flight that successfully ended the Gemini program. It proved to be a fortuitous selection, for during Project Gemini Aldrin became one of the key figures working on the problem of rendezvous of spacecraft in Earth or lunar orbit, and docking them together for spaceflight. Without these skills Apollo could not have been successfully completed. Aldin, with a Ph.D. in astronautics from Massachusetts Institute of Technology, was ideally qualified for this work, and his intellectual inclinations ensured that he carried out these tasks with enthusiasm. Systematically and laboriously, Aldrin worked to develop procedures and tools necessary to accomplish space rendezvous and docking. He was also a central figure in devising the methods necessary to carry out extravehicular activities (EVA) of astronauts outside their vehicles. That, too, was critical to the successful accomplishment of Apollo.

Aldrin was chosen as a member of the three-person Apollo 11 crew that landed on the Moon on 20 July 1969, fulfilling the mandate of President John F. Kennedy to send Americans to the Moon before the end of the decade. Aldrin was the second American to set foot on the lunar surface. He and Apollo 11 commander Neil A. Armstrong spent about twenty hours on the Moon before returning to the orbiting Apollo Command Module. The spacecraft and the lunar explorers returned to Earth on 24 July 1969.

In 1971 Aldrin returned to the Air Force and retired a year later. He wrote two important books about his activities in the U.S. space program. In *Return to Earth* (1970), Aldrin recounted the flight of Apollo 11. In the more broadly constructed *Men from Earth* (1989), Aldrin discussed the entire space race between the United States and the Soviet Union. He has been an important analyst of the space program since the 1960s. He lives near Los Angeles, California.

(July 1969) --- Astronaut Edwin E. Aldrin Jr. Aldrin was lunar module pilot of the Apollo 11 lunar landing mission.

Neil Alden Armstrong

Neil Alden Armstrong (1930-2012) was born on 5 August 1930 on his grandparents' farm near Wapakoneta, Ohio, to Stephen and Viola Armstrong. Because Armstrong's father was an auditor for the State of Ohio, Armstrong grew up in several communities, including Warren, Jefferson, Ravenna, St. Marys, and Upper Sandusky, before the family settled in Wapakoneta.

Armstrong developed an interest in flying at only age two when his father took him to the National Air Races in Cleveland, Ohio. His interest intensified when he went for his first airplane ride in a Ford Tri-Motor, a "Tin Goose," in Warren, Ohio, at age six. From that time on, he claimed an intense fascination with aviation.

At age fifteen, Armstrong began taking flying lessons at an airport north of Wapakoneta, working at various jobs in town and at the airport to earn the money for lessons in an Aeronca Champion airplane. By age sixteen, he had his student pilot's license, before he even passed his automobile driver's test and received that license and before he graduated from Blume High School in Wapakoneta in 1947.

Immediately after high school Armstrong received a scholarship from the U.S. Navy. He enrolled at Purdue University and began his studies of aeronautical engineering. In 1949, the Navy called him to active duty, where he became an aviator, and in 1950, he was sent to Korea. There he flew seventy-eight combat missions from the aircraft carrier U.S.S. Essex.

After mustering out of the Navy in 1952, Armstrong joined the National Advisory Committee for Aeronautics (NACA). His first assignment was at the NACA's Lewis Reserch Center, near Cleveland, Ohio. Lewis Flight Propulsion Laboratory (later NASA's Lewis Research Center, Cleveland, Ohio, and today the Glenn Research Center) in 1955. For the next seventeen years, he was an engineer, test pilot, astronaut, and administrator for the NACA and its successor agency, the National Aeronautics and Space Administration (NASA).

In the mid-1950s Armstrong transferred to NASA's Flight Research Center, Edwards, California, where he became a research pilot NACA's High-Speed Flight Station (today, NASA's Dryden Flight Research Center) at Edwards Air Force Base in California as an aeronautical research scientist and then as a pilot on many pioneering high-speed aircraft, including the well-known, 4,000-mph X-15. He flew over 200 different models of aircraft, including jets, rockets, helicopters, and gliders. While there he also pursued graduate studies, and received a master of science degree in aerospace engineering from the University of Southern California.

Armstrong transferred to astronaut status in 1962, one of nine NASA astronauts in the second class to be chosen. He moved to El Lago, Texas, near Houston's Manned Spacecraft Center, to begin his astronaut training. There he underwent four years of intensive training for the Apollo program to land an American on the Moon before the end of the decade.

On 16 March 1966, Armstrong flew his first space mission as command pilot of Gemini VIII with David Scott. During that mission Armstrong piloted the Gemini VIII spacecraft to a successful docking with an Agena target spacecraft already in orbit. While the docking went smoothly and the two craft orbited together, they began to pitch and roll wildly. Armstrong was able to undock the Gemini and used the retro rockets to regain control of his craft, but the astronauts had to make an emergency landing in the Pacific Ocean.

As spacecraft commander for Apollo 11, the first piloted lunar landing mission, Armstrong gained the distinction of being the first person to step on the surface of the Moon. On 16 July 1969, Armstrong, Michael Collins, and Edwin E. "Buzz" Aldrin began their trip to the Moon. Collins was the Command Module pilot and navigator for the mission. Aldrin, a systems expert, was the Lunar Module pilot and became the second person to walk on the Moon. As commander of Apollo 11, Armstrong piloted the Lunar Module to a safe landing on the Moon's surface. On 20 July 1969, at 10:56 p.m. EDT, Neil Armstrong stepped down onto the Moon and made his famous statement, "That's one small step for a man, one giant leap for mankind." Armstrong and Aldrin spent about two and one-half hours walking on the Moon collecting samples, doing experiments, and taking photographs. On 24 July 1969, the three men splashed down in the Pacific Ocean. They were picked up by the aircraft carrier, U.S.S. Hornet.

The three Apollo 11 astronauts were honored with a ticker tape parade in New York City soon after returning to Earth. Armstrong received the Medal of Freedom, the highest award offered to a U.S. civilian. Armstrong's other awards coming in the wake of the Apollo 11 mission included the NASA Distinguished Service Medal, the NASA Exceptional Service Medal, seventeen medals from other countries, and the Congressional Space Medal of Honor.

Armstrong subsequently held the position of Deputy Associate Administrator for Aeronautics, NASA Headquarters, Washington, D.C., in the early 1970s. In that position, he was responsible for the coordination and management of overall NASA research and technology work related to aeronautics.

After resigning from NASA in 1971, he became a professor of Aerospace Engineering at the University of Cincinnati from 1971 to 1979. During the years 1982-1992, Armstrong served as chairman of Computing Technologies for Aviation, Inc., in Charlottesville, Virginia. He then became chairman of the board of AIL Systems, Inc., an electronics systems company in Deer Park, New York. Armstrong died on Aug. 25, 2012 at the age of 82 due to complications relating to recent cardiovascular bypass procedures.

(July 1969) --- Astronaut Neil A. Armstrong. Armstrong was commander of Apollo 11 Lunar Landing Mission.

Michael Collins

Michael Collins (1930-) was born on October 30, 1930, in Rome, Italy. He later moved to Washington, D.C., where he graduated from St. Albans School. In 1952, he attended the U.S. Military Academy at West Point, New York, and received his bachelor of science degree.

Prior to joining NASA, Collins served as a fighter pilot and an experimental test pilot at the Air Force Flight Center, Edwards Air Force Base, California. From 1959 to1963 he logged more than 4,200 hours of flying time.

In October 1963, Michael Collins became one of the third group of astronauts named by NASA. He served as a pilot on the three-day Gemini X mission, launched July 18, 1966. During this mission, he set a world altitude record and became the nation's third spacewalker while completing two extravehicular activities (EVA).

His second flight was as Command Module pilot of the historic Apollo 11 mission in July 1969. He remained in lunar orbit while Neil Armstrong and Buzz Aldrin became the first people to walk on the Moon. His role in the Apollo mission earned him many awards and accolades, including the Presidential Medal for Freedom in 1969.

In January 1970, Collins left NASA to become the Assistant Secretary of State for Public Affairs. A year later he joined the Smithsonian Institution as the Director of the National Air and Space Museum, where he remained for seven years. While in this position, he was responsible for the construction of the new museum building, which opened to the public in July 1976, ahead of schedule and below its budgeted cost. In April 1978, Collins became Under Secretary of the Smithsonian Institution.

In 1980, he became the Vice President of the LTV Aerospace and Defense Company, resigning in 1985 to start his own firm.

Collins has completed two spaceflights, logging 266 hours in space, of which 1 hour and 27 minutes was spent in EVA. He has written about his experiences in the space program in several books, including *Carrying the Fire* and *Flying to the Moon and other Strange Places*. In 1988, he wrote *Liftoff: the Story of America's Adventure in Space*. Today he is an aerospace consultant and writer.

(July 1969) --- Astronaut Michael Collins.

(10 Jan. 1969) --- These three astronauts have been selected by NASA as the prime crew of the Apollo 11 lunar landing mission. Left to right, are Edwin E. Aldrin Jr., lunar module pilot; Neil A. Armstrong, commander; and Michael Collins, command module pilot. They are photographed in front of a lunar module mock-up beside Building 1 following a press conference in the MSC Auditorium.

3 PRE LAUNCH – CREW & SUPPORT

With 18 days before launch, Apollo 11 Command Module (CM) pilot Michael Collins practices docking hatch removal from CM simulator at NASA Johnson Space Center.

(25 Feb. 1969) --- These two Apollo 11 crew astronauts study rock samples during a geological field trip to the Quitman Mountains area near the Fort Quitman ruins in far west Texas. Neil A. Armstrong (in background) is the Apollo 11 commander; and Edwin E. Aldrin Jr. is the lunar module pilot.

Apollo 11 crew member Michael Collins appears calm after suiting up activities for his participation in the countdown demonstration test aboard the Apollo 11 space craft along with astronauts Aldrin and Armstrong.

The Apollo 11 crew performs a walk-through egress test. The hands-on test was in preparation for the first manned lunar landing mission.

(24 May 1969) --- The prime crew of the Apollo 11 lunar landing mission relaxes on the deck of the NASA Motor Vessel Retriever prior to participating in water egress training in the Gulf of Mexico. Left to right, are astronauts Edwin E. Aldrin Jr., lunar module pilot; Neil A. Armstrong, commander; and Michael Collins, command module pilot. In the background is Apollo Boilerplate 1102 which was used in the training exercise.

(6 May 1968) --- Astronaut Neil A. Armstrong, Apollo 11 mission commander, floats safely to the ground. The Lunar Landing Research Vehicle (LLRV) exploded only seconds before while Armstrong was rehearsing a lunar landing at Ellington Air Force Base near the Manned Spacecraft Center (MSC). The photo is a blowup of 16mm documentary motion picture recorded during the mishap.

(18 April 1969) --- Suited astronaut Neil A. Armstrong, wearing an Extravehicular Mobility Unit (EMU), participates in lunar surface simulation training on April 18, 1969, in Building 9, Manned Spacecraft Center. Armstrong is the prime crew commander of the Apollo 11 lunar landing mission. Here, he practices scooping up a lunar sample.

(22 April 1969) Two members of the Apollo 11 lunar landing mission participate in a simulation of deploying and using lunar tools on the surface of the moon. The rehearsal took place during a training exercise in building 9 on April 22, 1969. Astronaut Edwin E. Aldrin Jr. (on left), lunar module pilot, uses a scoop and tongs to pick up samples. Astronaut Neil A. Armstrong, Apollo 11 commander, holds the bag to receive the sample. In the background is a Lunar Module (LM) mock-up.

(22 April 1969) --- Astronaut Neil A. Armstrong, wearing an Extravehicular Mobility Unit, participates in a simulation of deploying and using lunar tools on the surface of the moon during a training exercise in Building 9 on April 22, 1969. Armstrong is the commander of the Apollo 11 lunar landing mission. In the background is a Lunar Module mock-up.

(18 April 1969) --- Suited astronaut Neil A. Armstrong, wearing an Extravehicular Mobility Unit (EMU), participates in lunar surface simulation training on April 18, 1969 in building 9, Manned Spacecraft Center (MSC). Armstrong is prime crew commander of the Apollo 11 lunar landing mission. Here, he is opening a sample return container. On the right is the Modular Equipment Stowage Assembly (MESA) and the Lunar Module (LM) mock-up.

(22 April 1969) --- Astronaut Neil A. Armstrong, wearing an Extravehicular Mobility Unit (EMU), participates in a simulation of deploying and using lunar tools, on the surface of the moon, during a training exercise in Building 9 on April 22, 1969. Armstrong, commander of the Apollo 11 lunar landing mission, is holding sample bags. On the left is the Lunar Module (LM) mock-up.

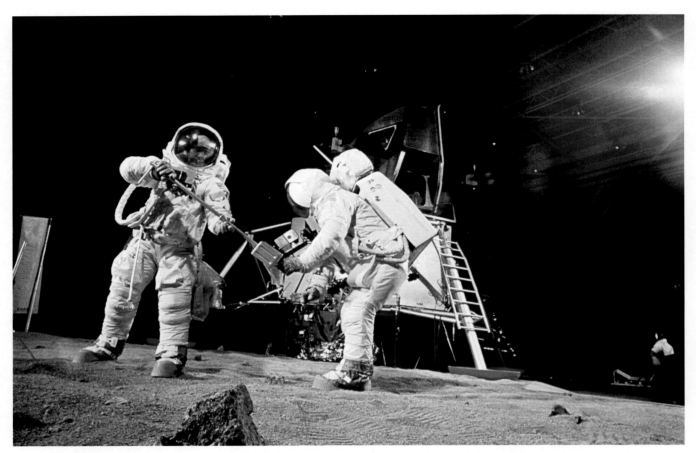

(22 April 1969) --- Two members of the Apollo 11 lunar landing mission participate in a simulation of deploying and using lunar tools, on the surface of the moon, during a training exercise in Building 9 on April 22, 1969. Astronaut Edwin E. Aldrin Jr. (on left), lunar module pilot, uses a scoop to pick up a sample. Astronaut Neil A. Armstrong, Apollo 11 commander, holds bag to receive sample. In the background is a Lunar Module (LM) mock-up. Both crewmembers are wearing Extravehicular Mobility Units (EMU).

(22 April 1969) --- Astronaut Edwin E. Aldrin Jr., wearing an Extravehicular Mobility Unit (EMU), simulates deploying the Solar Wind Composition (SWC) experiment, on the surface of the moon, during a training exercise in Building 9 on April 22, 1969. The SWC is a component of the Early Apollo Scientific Experiment Package (EASEP). Aldrin is the lunar module pilot of the Apollo 11 lunar landing mission.

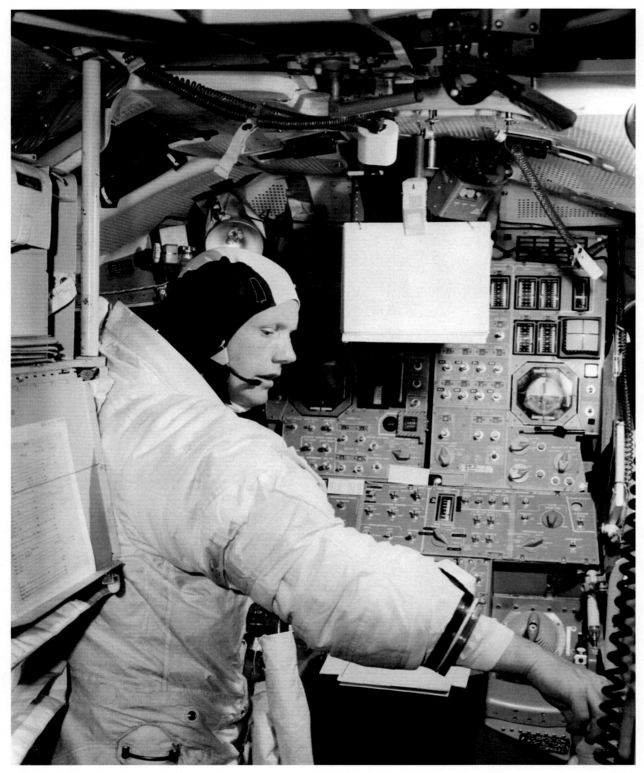

(19 June 1969) --- Astronaut Neil A. Armstrong, Apollo 11 commander, participates in simulation training in preparation for the scheduled lunar landing mission. He is in the Apollo Lunar Module Mission Simulator in the Kennedy Space Center (KSC) Flight Crew Training Building.

Neil A. Armstrong, commander for the Apollo 11 moon-landing mission, practices for the historic event in a lunar module simulator in the Flight Crew Training Building at Kennedy.

(22 April 1969) --- Astronaut Neil A. Armstrong, wearing an Extravehicular Mobility Unit (EMU), participates in a simulation of deploying and using lunar tools, on the surface of the moon, during a training exercise in Building 9 on April 22, 1969. Armstrong is the commander of the Apollo 11 lunar landing mission. He is using a scoop to place the sample into bag. On the right is a Lunar Module (LM) mock-up.

(April 1969) --- Astronaut Neil A. Armstrong, wearing an Extravehicular Mobility Unit (EMU), deploys a lunar surface television camera during lunar surface simulation training in Building 9, Manned Spacecraft Center (MSC). Armstrong is the prime crew commander of the Apollo 11 lunar landing mission.

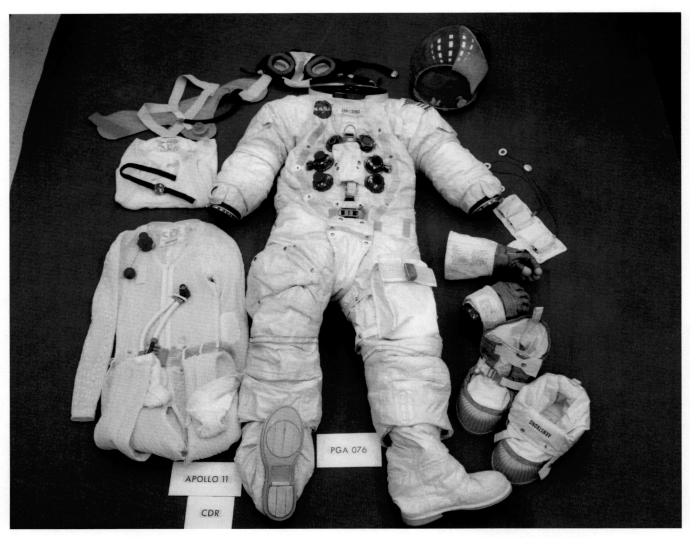

This pre-flight photo shows Neil's suit in its lunar surface configuration, which includes the Liquid Cooled Garment at the left and the EVA (Extra-vehicular) gloves and moon boots at the right.

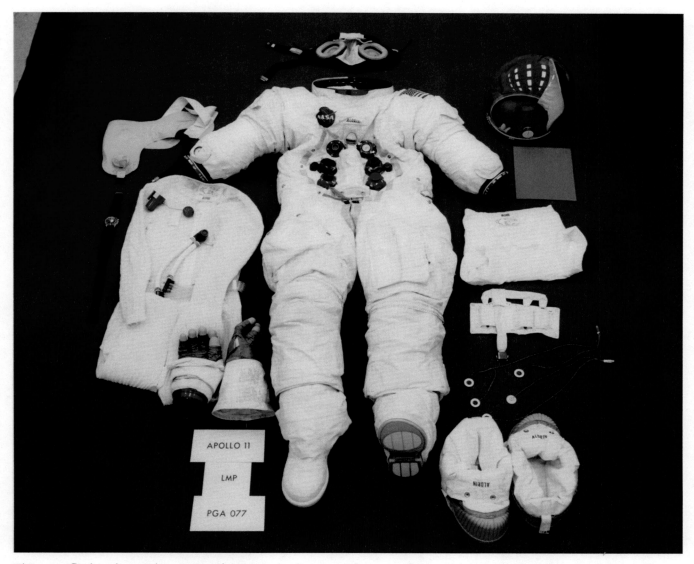

This pre-flight photo shows Buzz's suit in its lunar surface configuration. Note that the sewn-on cuff checklist can be seen on the wrist cover of Buzz's left glove, the one closest to the right suit leg.

This group portrait was taken at Philmont Scout Ranch in northeastern New Mexico during a 3-6 June 1964 geology field trip. From left to right, they are: Pete Conrad, Buzz Aldrin, Dick Gordon, Ted Freeman, Charlie Bassett, Walt Cunningham, Neil Armstrong, Donn Eisele, Rusty Schweikhart (behind Eisele), Jim Lovell, Mike Collins (partly hidden behind Lovell), Elliot See, Gene Cernan (behind See), Ed White, Roger Chaffee, Gordon Cooper, C.C. Williams (behind Cooper), Bill Anders, Dave Scott, Al Bean.

Dr. Wernher von Braun pauses in front of the Saturn V vehicle being readied for the historic Apollo 11 lunar landing mission. The Saturn V vehicle was developed by the Marshall Space Flight Center in Huntsville, Alabama under the direction of von Braun.

4 PRE-LAUNCH - THE SATURN V ROCKET

Rollout of the Apollo 11 Saturn V rocket from the Vehicle Assembly Building to the launch pad.

The Saturn V was a rocket NASA built to send people to the moon. (The V in the name is the Roman numeral five.) The Saturn V was a type of rocket called a Heavy Lift Vehicle. That means it was very powerful. It was the most powerful rocket that had ever flown successfully. The Saturn V was used in the Apollo program in the 1960s and 1970s. It also was used to launch the Skylab space station.

How Big Was the Saturn V?

The Saturn V rocket was 111 meters (363 feet) tall, about the height of a 36-story-tall building, and 18 meters (60 feet) taller than the Statue of Liberty. Fully fueled for liftoff, the Saturn V weighed 2.8 million kilograms (6.2 million pounds), the weight of about 400 elephants. The rocket generated 34.5 million newtons (7.6 million pounds) of **thrust** at launch, creating more power than 85 Hoover Dams. A car that gets 48 kilometers (30 miles) to the gallon could drive around the world around 800 times with the amount of fuel the Saturn V used for a lunar landing mission. It could launch about 118,000 kilograms (130 tons) into Earth orbit. That's about as much weight as 10 school buses. The Saturn V could launch about 43,500 kilograms (50 tons) to the moon. That's about the same as four school buses.

What Is the History of the Saturn V?

The Saturn V was developed at NASA's Marshall Space Flight Center in Huntsville, Ala. It was one of three types of Saturn rockets NASA built. Two smaller rockets, the Saturn I (1) and IB (1b), were used to launch humans into Earth orbit. The Saturn V sent them beyond Earth orbit to the moon. The first Saturn V was launched in 1967. It was called Apollo 4. Apollo 6 followed in 1968. Both of these rockets were launched without crews. These launches tested the Saturn V rocket.

The first Saturn V launched with a crew was Apollo 8. On this mission, astronauts orbited the moon but did not land. On Apollo 9, the crew tested the Apollo moon lander by flying it in Earth orbit without landing. On Apollo 10, the Saturn V launched the lunar lander to the moon. The crew tested the lander in space but did not land it on the moon. In 1969, Apollo 11 was the first mission to land astronauts on the moon. Saturn V rockets also made it possible for astronauts to land on the moon on Apollo 12, 14, 15, 16 and 17. On Apollo 13, the Saturn V lifted the crew into space, but a problem prevented them from being able to land on the moon. That problem was not with the Saturn V, but with the Apollo spacecraft. The last Saturn V was launched in 1973, without a crew. It was used to launch the Skylab space station into Earth orbit.

How Did the Saturn V Work?

The Saturn V that launched the Skylab space station only had two **stages**. The Saturn V rockets used for the Apollo missions had three stages. Each stage would burn its engines until it was out of fuel and would then separate from the rocket. The engines on the next stage would fire, and the rocket would continue into space. The first stage had the most powerful engines, since it had the challenging task of lifting the fully fueled rocket off the ground. The first stage lifted the rocket to an altitude of about 68 kilometers (42 miles). The second stage carried it from there almost into orbit. The third stage placed the Apollo spacecraft into Earth orbit and pushed it toward the moon. The first two stages fell into the ocean after separation. The third stage either stayed in space or hit the moon.

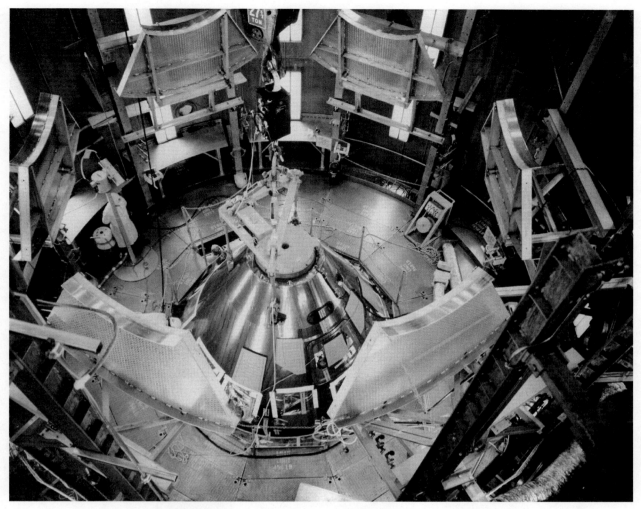

The command and service modules for Apollo 11 are installed in the altitude chamber of the Manned Spacecraft Operations Building at KSC.

A crane lifts the S-IC stage in preparation for stacking on a mobile launcher within the VAB's High Bay 1. Photo filed 21 February 1969.

This photo shows the Apollo 11 Command-and-Service Module being mated to the spacecraft adapter. Photo filed 1 May 1969.

The S-1C booster for the Apollo 11 Saturn V waits inside the Vehicle Assembly Building at NASA's Kennedy Space Center.

Here, the Instrument Unit is lowered into place atop the third stage of the Saturn V launch vehicle in the Vehicle Assembly Building at Kennedy. Designed at NASA's Marshall Space Flight Center, the Instrument Unit served as the "nerve center" for the Saturn V, providing guidance and control, command and sequence of vehicle functions, telemetry and environmental control. Marshall designed, developed and managed the production of the Saturn V rocket that took astronauts to the moon.

This photo shows the Saturn V's second stage being lowered into place atop the first stage in the Vehicle Assembly Building at NASA's Kennedy Space Center. The Saturn V rocket was designed, managed and built by NASA's Marshall Space Flight Center.

(11 April 1969) --- Interior view of the Kennedy Space Center's (KSC) Manned Spacecraft Operations Building showing Apollo Spacecraft 107 Command and Service Modules (CSM) being moved from work stand 134 for mating to Spacecraft Lunar Module Adapter (SLA) 14.

The Transporter nears the top of the five percent incline at Launch Complex 39A with the Apollo 11 Saturn V.

During a nighttime training session, a multiple exposure captures the movement of the Lunar Excursion Module Simulator (LEMS). The LEMS was a manned rocket-powered vehicle used to familiarize the Apollo astronauts with the handling characteristics of a lunar-landing type vehicle.

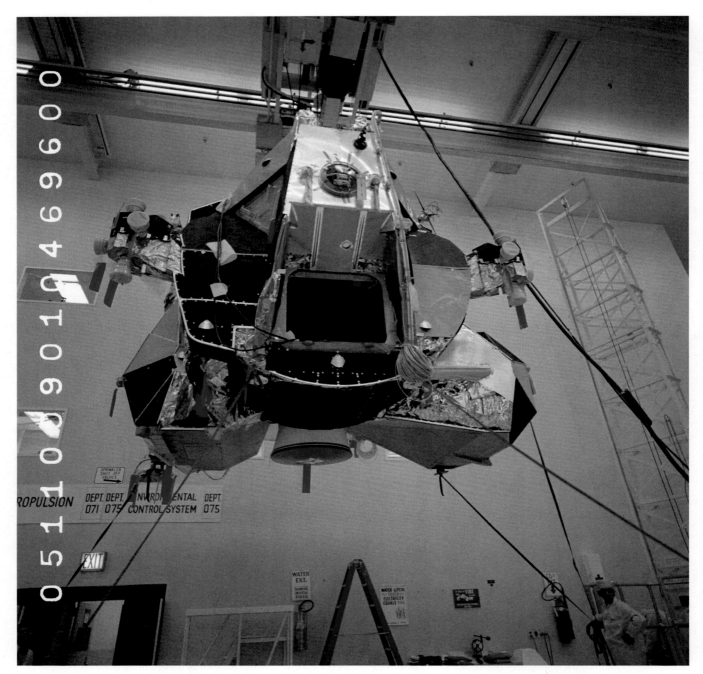

(4 Jan. 1969) --- Lunar Module (LM) 5 ascent stage in Final Assembly Area on overhead hoist being moved to dolly for roll-out inspection. LM-5 will be flown on the Apollo 11 lunar landing mission.

(4 April 1969) --- Interior view of the Kennedy Space Center's (KSC) Manned Spacecraft Operations Building showing Lunar Module (LM) 5 being moved from work stand for mating with its Spacecraft Lunar Module Adapter (SLA). LM-5 is scheduled to be flown on the Apollo 11 lunar landing mission.

Aerial view of the Apollo 11 Saturn V rollout from the Vehicle Assembly Building. 20 May 1969.

Aboard a Saturn V launch vehicle, the Apollo 11 mission launched from The Kennedy Space Center, Florida on July 16, 1969 and safely returned to Earth on July 24, 1969. The space vehicle is shown here during the rollout for launch preparation.

The Apollo 11 Command/Service Module (CSM) are being mated to the Saturn V Lunar Module Adapter on April 11, 1969.

A 1964 photo shows the Lunar Landing Research Vehicle (LLRV), affectionately dubbed the "flying bedstead" in flight at Edwards Air Force Base in California. NASA used the LLRV to simulate the Apollo lunar landings. Apollo 11 Commander Neil Armstrong had a close call in one of these machines in 1968, ejecting safely just seconds before a crash.

View of Apollo 11 from the tower, with the Mobile Service Structure opposite.

The 402-foot-tall mobile service structure is moved away from the Apollo 11 spacecraft at Kennedy's Launch Pad 39A. The move was made during the Countdown Demonstration Test with Apollo 11 astronauts Neil A. Armstrong, Michael Collins and Edwin E. Aldrin Jr.

High-angle view of the White Room and the Apollo 11 Command-and-Service Module. Photo filed 11 July 1969.

5 APOLLO 11 LAUNCH EVENTS

The crewmen of the Apollo 11 lunar landing mission leave the Kennedy Space Center's (KSC) Manned Spacecraft Operations Building (MSOB) during the prelaunch countdown. Astronauts Neil A. Armstrong, commander; Michael Collins, command module pilot; and Edwin E. Aldrin Jr., lunar module pilot, ride the special transport van over to Launch Complex 39A where their spacecraft awaited them. Liftoff was at 9:32 a.m. (EDT), July 16, 1969.

(16 July 1969) --- The crew of the Apollo 11 lunar landing mission arrives atop Pad A, Launch Complex 39, Kennedy Space Center, during the Apollo 11 prelaunch countdown. Leading is astronaut Neil A. Armstrong, commander. He was followed by astronauts Michael Collins, command module pilot. Technician follows directly behind Armstrong and Collins.

The huge, 363-feet tall Apollo 11 (Spacecraft 107/Lunar Module 5/Saturn 506) space vehicle is launched from Pad A, Launch Complex 39, Kennedy Space Center (KSC), at 9:32 a.m. (EDT), July 16, 1969. Aboard the Apollo 11 spacecraft were astronauts Neil A. Armstrong, commander; Michael Collins, command module pilot; and Edwin E. Aldrin Jr., lunar module pilot. Apollo 11 is the United States' first lunar landing mission. This view of the liftoff was taken by a camera mounted on the mobile launch tower. While astronauts Armstrong and Aldrin descend in the Lunar Module (LM) "Eagle" to explore the Sea of Tranquility region of the moon, astronaut Collins will remain with the Command and Service Modules (CSM) "Columbia" in lunar orbit.

(16 July 1969) --- Another view of the launch.

(16 July 1969) --- Another view of the launch.

(16 July 1969) --- Another view of the launch.

(16 July 1969) --- A fish-eye lens view of the launch of the huge, 363-feet-tall Apollo 11 (Spacecraft 107/Lunar Module 5/Saturn 506) space vehicle from Pad A, Launch Complex 39, Kennedy Space Center (KSC), at 9:32 a.m. (EDT), July 16, 1969. Aboard the Apollo 11 spacecraft were astronauts Neil A. Armstrong, commander; Michael Collins, command module pilot; and Edwin E. Aldrin Jr., lunar module pilot. Apollo 11 is the United States' first lunar landing mission. This photograph of the liftoff was taken by a camera mounted on the mobile launch tower.

(16 July 1969) --- Another view of the launch.

The Apollo 11 Saturn V lifts off with astronauts Neil A. Armstrong, Michael Collins and Edwin E. Aldrin Jr. at 9:32 a.m. EDT July 16, 1969, from Kennedy's Launch Complex 39A.

(16 July 1969) --- Another view of the launch.

The American flag heralded the launch of Apollo 11, the first Lunar landing mission, on July 16, 1969. The massive Saturn V rocket lifted off from NASA's Kennedy Space Center with astronauts Neil A. Armstrong, Michael Collins, and Edwin "Buzz" Aldrin at 9:32 a.m. EDT. Four days later, on July 20, Armstrong and Aldrin landed on the Moon's surface.

(July 16, 1969) The Apollo 11 Saturn V space vehicle climbs toward orbit after liftoff from Pad 39A at 9:32 a.m. EDT on July 16, 1969. In 2 1/2 minutes of powered flight, the S-IC booster lifts the vehicle to an altitude of about 39 miles some 55 miles downrange. This photo was taken with a 70mm telescopic camera mounted in an Air Force EC-135N plane. Onboard are astronauts Neil A. Armstrong, Michael Collins and Edwin E. Aldrin, Jr.

(16 July 1969) --- A 70mm Airborne Lightweight Optical Tracking System (ALOTS) took this picture. ALOTS tracking camera mounted on an Air Force EC-135 aircraft flying at about 40,000 feet altitude photographed this event in the early moments of the Apollo 11 launch. The 7.6 million-pound thrust Saturn V (S-1C) first stage boosts the space vehicle to an altitude of 36.3 nautical miles at 50.6 nautical miles downrange in 2 minutes 40.8 seconds. The S-1C stage separates at 2 minutes 41.6 seconds after liftoff.

Launch control team member Jerry Croley writes, "We were listening to Vice President Spiro Agnew, who gave us a pep talk about an hour after the launch. I was stationed at console BE-17 with call sign C2HU. This was the SII LH Propellant Tanking Computer System, the controller that kept the LH level at the correct Flight Mass specified for the mission. It simply monitored the level through a capacitance probe and added LH as the LH evaporated following the filling by the Propellants section and through pressurization, after which there was no boil off. Our section was an Elec section working alongside the Mechs who managed the tank farms and overall propellant handling. (In the photo), I am standing (128k on the edge of the A level in front of the A level consoles (the side away from the window). Unfortunately, I cannot recognize any of the people from row BE." Deke Slayton, in a dark shirt with no tie, is six from the right in the second row, and Alan Shepard is next but one to Slayton's right. Kipp Teague notes that the clocks on the wall show Local (time) 10:25, Projected Launch (time) 9:32, and Accumulated Hold 12:00 (meaning 'none'. "As evidenced by the clocks, the photo was taken 53 minutes after liftoff." 16 July 1969.

6 IN SPACE

This interior view of the Apollo 11 Lunar Module (LM) shows astronaut Edwin E. Aldrin Jr., lunar module pilot, during the lunar landing mission. This picture was taken by astronaut Neil A. Armstrong, commander. While astronauts Armstrong and Aldrin descended in the LM "Eagle" to explore the Sea of Tranquility region of the moon, astronaut Michael Collins, command module pilot, remained with the Command and Service Modules (CSM) "Columbia" in lunar orbit.

The Apollo 11 Lunar Module ascent stage, with astronauts Neil A. Armstrong and Edwin E. Aldrin Jr. aboard, is photographed from the Command and Service Modules (CSM) during rendezvous in lunar orbit. The Lunar Module (LM) was making its docking approach to the CSM. Astronaut Michael Collins remained with the CSM in lunar orbit while the other two crewmen explored the lunar surface. The large, dark-colored area in the background is Smyth's Sea, centered at 85 degrees east longitude and 2 degrees south latitude on the lunar surface (nearside). This view looks west. The Earth rises above the lunar horizon.

(21 July 1969) --- The Apollo 11 Lunar Module (LM) ascent stage, with astronauts Neil A. Armstrong and Edwin E. Aldrin Jr. onboard, is photographed from the Command and Services Modules (CSM) in lunar orbit. This view is looking west with the Earth rising above the lunar horizon. Astronaut Michael Collins remained with the CSM in lunar orbit while Armstrong and Aldrin explored the moon. The LM is approaching from below. The maze area in the background is Smyth's Sea. At right center is International Astronomical Union crater No. 189.

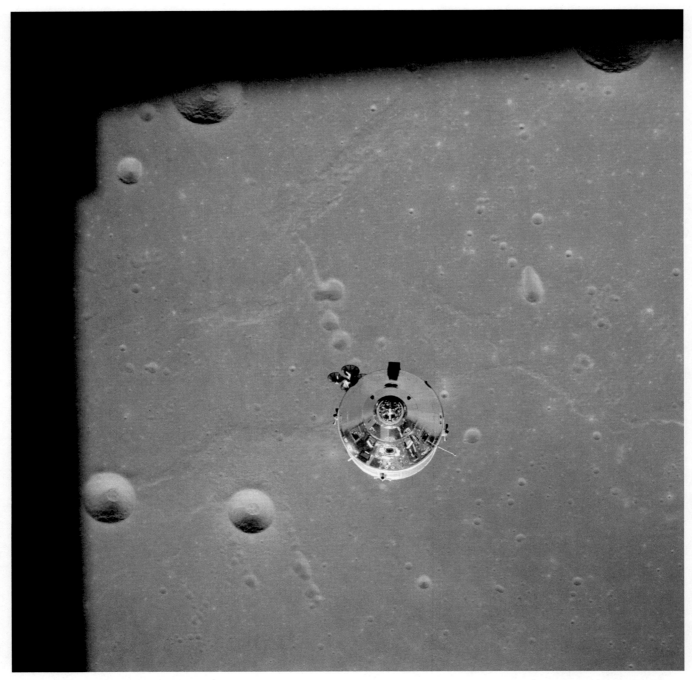

Command Module Columbia over Craters Taruntius K, Taruntius P, and Dorsum Cayeux in north central Mare Fecunditatis (Sea of Fertility). The coordinates of the center of the picture are 51 degrees east longitude and 1 degree north latitude. About half of the crater Taruntius G is visible in the upper left corner of the picture. Research by Danny Caes. Markus Mehring notes that the two craters partly visible at the top are Anvil and Taruntius H.

Post-undocking view of the CSM during the separation sequence, with the eastern part of the Sea of Fertility (Mare Fecunditatis) about 195 km below. North is to the right. The two spacecraft undocked at about 100:12:03

(20 July 1969) --- The Apollo 11 Command and Service Modules (CSM) are photographed from the Lunar Module (LM) in lunar orbit during the Apollo 11 lunar landing mission. The lunar surface below is in the north central Sea of Fertility. The coordinates of the center of the picture are 51 degrees east longitude and 1 degree north latitude. About half of the crater Taruntius G is visible in the lower left corner of the picture. Part of Taruntius H can be seen at lower right.

LM pulling away during separation.

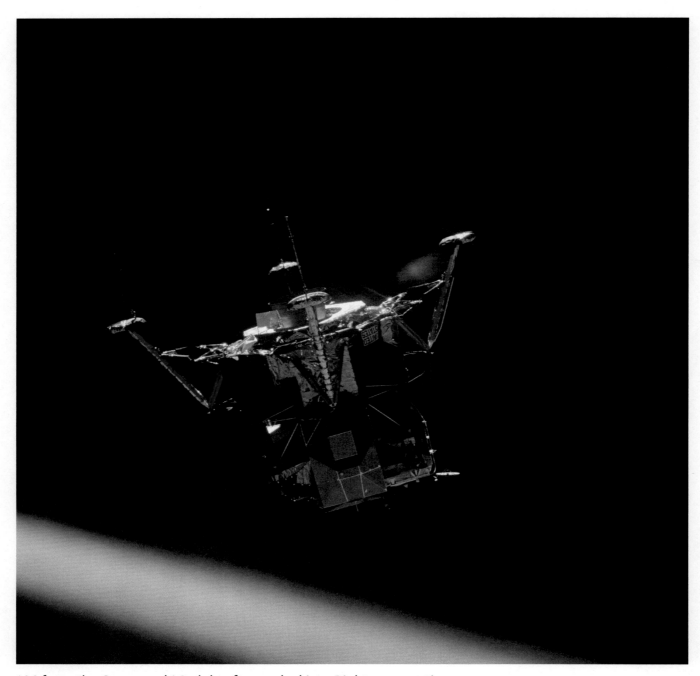

LM from the Command Module after undocking. Right yaw continues.

LM from the Command Module after undocking. The ladder strut in on Mike's right. There has been sufficent roll that the bottom on the LM is no longer visible. We are looking at Buzz's side of the LM.

Earth. Front of the LM. Adjusting LM roll. Babcock cut off by CM window frame. Mare Smythii beyond.

Lunar surface in focus. Kiing Crater to the right of the thrusters

View of Mare Fecunditatis from Armstrong's window. The two craters close together in the middle distance are Messier and Messier A, with light-colored rays extending westward from Messier A, the more distant of the two.

The Apollo 11 Lunar Module Eagle, in a landing configuration was photographed in lunar orbit from the Command and Service Module Columbia. Inside the module were Commander Neil A. Armstrong and Lunar Module Pilot Buzz Aldrin. The long rod-like protrusions under the landing pods are lunar surface sensing probes.

(20 July 1969) --- The Apollo 11 Lunar Module (LM), in a lunar landing configuration, is photographed in lunar orbit from the Command and Service Modules (CSM). Inside the LM were astronauts Neil A. Armstrong, commander, and Edwin E. Aldrin Jr., lunar module pilot. Astronaut Michael Collins, command module pilot, remained with the CSM in lunar orbit while Armstrong and Aldrin descended in the LM to explore the lunar surface.

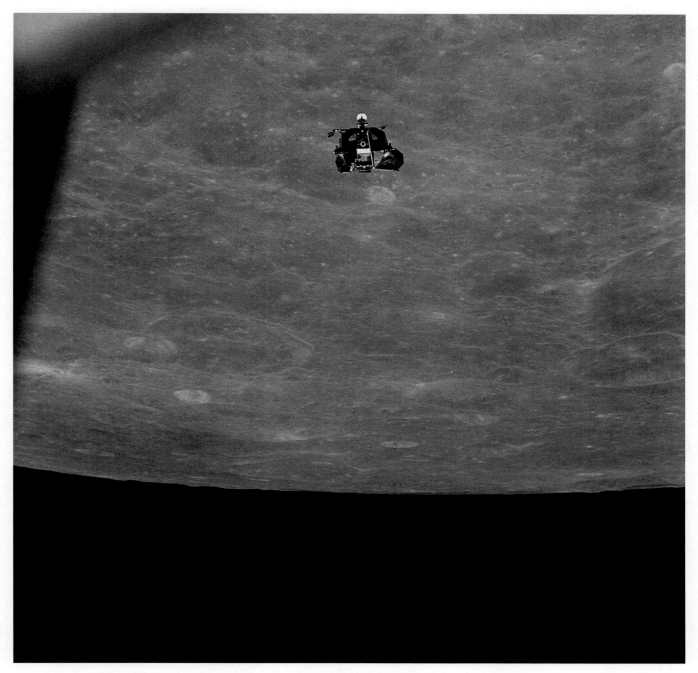

(21 July 1969) --- The Apollo 11 Lunar Module (LM) ascent stage, with astronauts Neil A. Armstrong and Edwin E. Aldrin Jr. aboard, is photographed from the Command and Service Modules (CSM) in lunar orbit. Astronaut Michael Collins, command module pilot, remained with the CSM in lunar orbit while Armstrong and Aldrin explored the moon. The LM is approaching from below. The coordinates of the center of the lunar terrain seen below is located at 102 degrees east longitude and 1 degree north latitude.

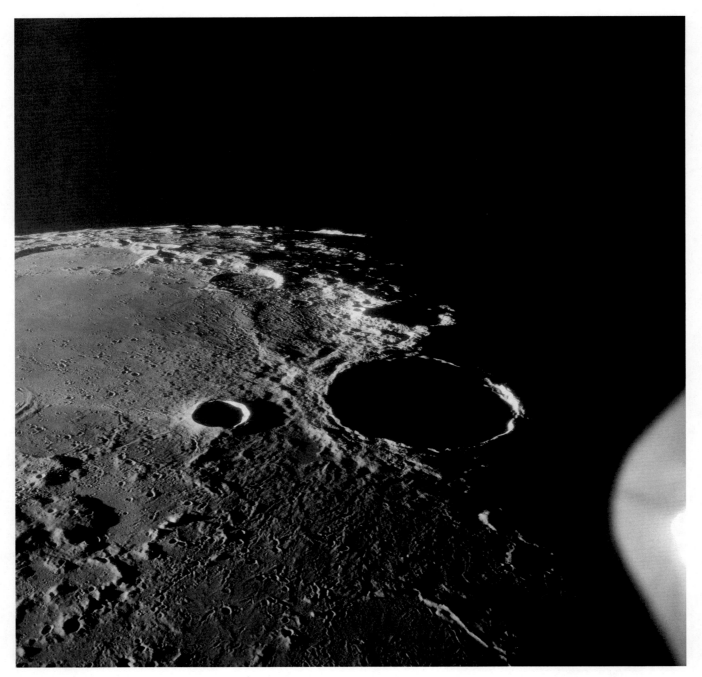

(20 July 1969) --- An Apollo 11 oblique view of the large crater Theophilus located at the northwest edge of the Sea of Nectar on the lunar nearside. Theophilus is about 60 statute miles in diameter. The smooth area is Mare Nectaris. The smaller crater Madler, about 14 statute miles in diameter, is located to the east of Theophilus. Visible in the background are the large crater Fracastorius and the smaller crater Beaumont. The coordinates of the center of this photograph are 29 degrees east longitude and 11 degrees south latitude.

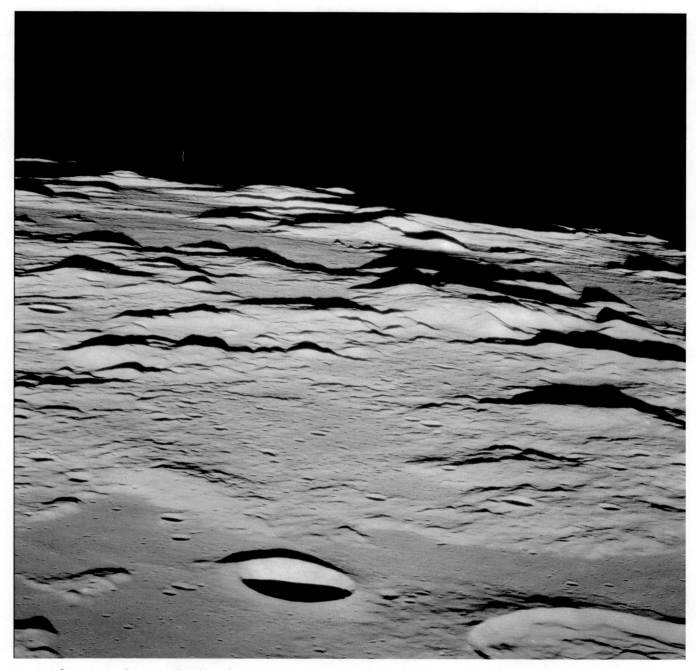

View of Moon,Sabine and Schmidt Craters. This image is part of a west looking oblique sequence of images taken from the Command and Service Module (CSM) as it traveled at approximately 60 nautical miles (NM) orbital altitude above the Moon during the Apollo 11 Mission. This sequence commences at 35 degrees East Longitude and continues to the nearside lunar terminator. Original film magazine was labeled P. Film Type: 3400 Panatomic-X Black/White taken with a 250mm lens. Approximate Photo Scale 1:1,126,100. Principal Point Latitude 1 degree North and Longitude 16 degrees East. Forward overlap: 86%. Sun angle is Low. Approximate Tilt Minimum is 65 degrees,Maximum is 70 degrees. Tilt direction is West (W).

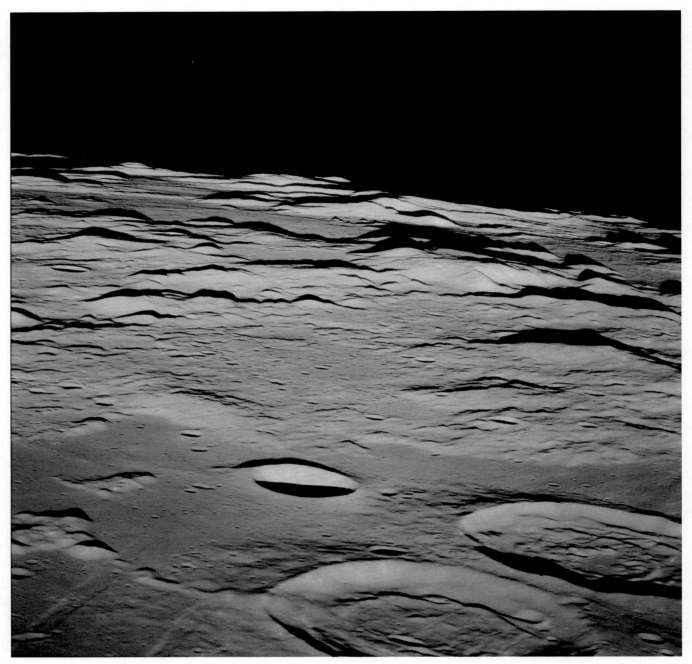

View of Moon,Sabine and Ritter Craters. The twin Craters Sabine and Ritter are in the right foreground and the Crater Schmidt is in the central foreground. This image is part of a west looking oblique sequence of images taken from the Command and Service Module (CSM) as it traveled at approximately 60 nautical miles (NM) orbital altitude above the Moon during the Apollo 11 Mission. This sequence commences at 35 degrees East Longitude and continues to the nearside lunar terminator. Original film magazine was labeled P. Film Type: 3400 Panatomic-X Black/White taken with a 250mm lens. Approximate Photo Scale 1:1,126,100. Principal Point Latitude 1 degree North and Longitude 17 degrees East. Forward overlap: 85%. Sun angle is Low. Approximate Tilt Minimum is 65 degrees,Maximum is 70 degrees. Tilt direction is West (W).

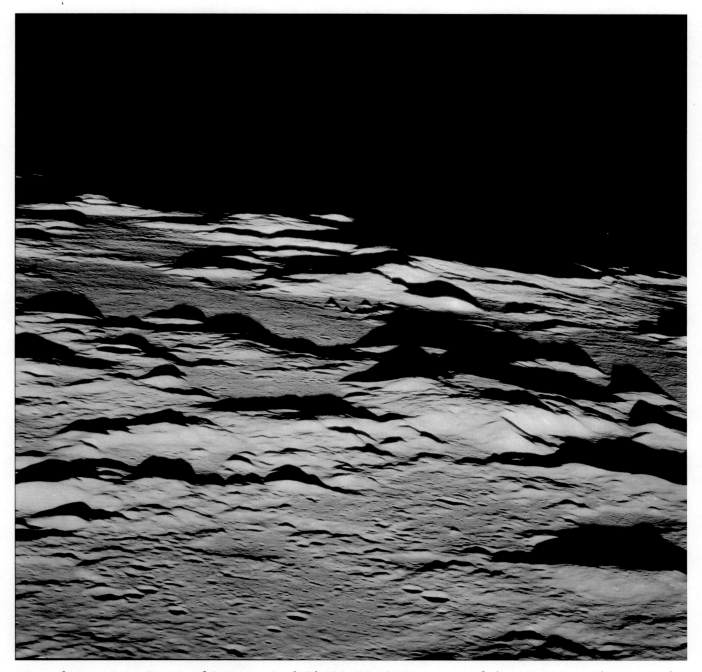

View of Moon,Start Target of Opportunity (TO) 132. TO 132 is an area of elongate cratered cones and irregular domes of probable volcanic origin. This image is part of a west looking oblique sequence of images taken from the Command and Service Module (CSM) as it traveled at approximately 60 nautical miles (NM) orbital altitude above the Moon during the Apollo 11 Mission. This sequence commences at 35 degrees East Longitude and continues to the nearside lunar terminator. Original film magazine was labeled P. Film Type: 3400 Panatomic-X Black/White taken with a 250mm lens. Approximate Photo Scale 1:1,227,800. Principal Point Latitude 1 degree North and Longitude 14 degrees East. Forward overlap: 85%. Sun angle is Low. Approximate Tilt Minimum is 65 degrees,Maximum is 70 degrees. Tilt direction is West (W).

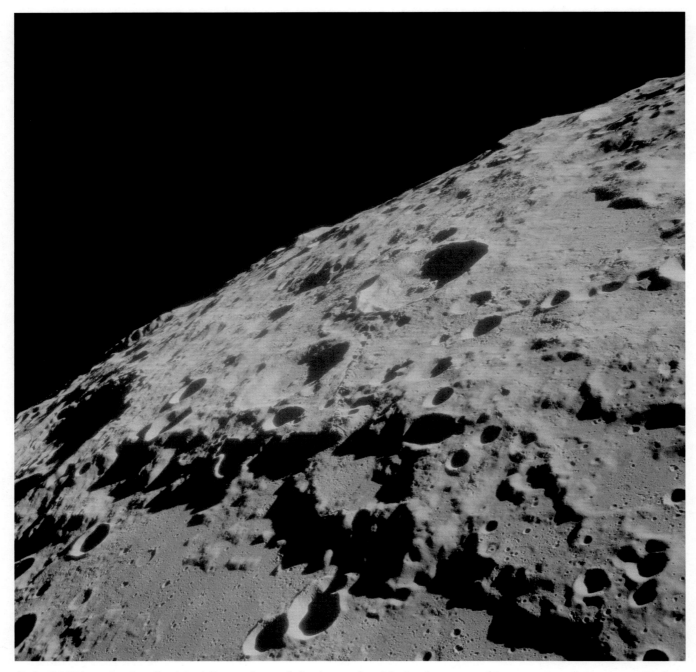

(July 1969) --- An Apollo 11 oblique view of the lunar farside in the area of International Astronomical Union crater No. 312, which is about 30 statute miles in diameter. The center of the photograph is located at 164 degrees west longitude and 8 degrees south latitude. The sharp shadows indicate that the picture was taken at a low sun angle.

(20 July 1969) --- The rough terrain in this photograph is typical of the farside of the moon. This lunar picture was taken from the Apollo 11 spacecraft during the lunar landing mission. About one-half of International Astronomical Union (I.A.U.) crater NO. 308 is visible at upper right. The coordinates of the center of I.A.U. crater NO. 308 are 179.3 degrees east longitude and 6 degrees south latitude. While astronauts Neil A. Armstrong, commander; and Edwin E. Aldrin Jr., lunar module pilot; descended in the Lunar Module (LM) "Eagle" to explore the moon, astronaut Michael Collins, command module pilot, remained with the Command and Service Modules (CSM) in lunar orbit.

Shadowed crater Icarus in foreground with central peak lit by setting Sun. View south towards Amici T.

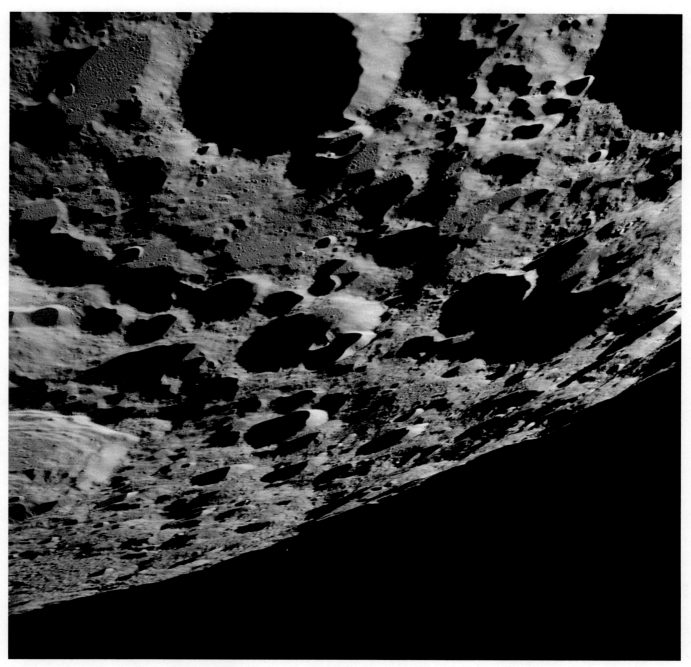

Crater Daedalus G near centre of frame. Daedalus is cut off at edge of image.

(16-24 July 1969) --- An oblique of the Crater Daedalus on the lunar farside as seen from the Apollo 11 spacecraft in lunar orbit. The view looks southwest. Daedalus (formerly referred to as I.A.U. Crater No. 308) is located at 179 degrees east longitude and 5.5 degrees south latitude. Daedalus has a diameter of about 50 statute miles. This is a typical scene showing the rugged terrain on the farside of the moon. While astronauts Neil A. Armstrong, commander, and Edwin E. Aldrin Jr., lunar module pilot, descended in the Lunar Module (LM) "Eagle" to explore the Sea of Tranquility region of the moon, astronaut Michael Collins, command module pilot, remained with the Command and Service Modules (CSM) "Columbia" in lunar orbit.

(July 1969) --- This is a northeasterly, low-oblique view of an unmanned crater and highland area on the lunar farside, as photographed from Apollo 11. The center of the picture is located at the 167 degrees east longitude and 6 degrees north latitude. This area of the moon lies just east of International Astronomical Union crater

Messier Crater (left) and Messier A. Messier was probbly formed by an impactor which struck the Moon at a very shallow angle. Messier is located at 47.6 E and 1.9 S and is about 9 x 11 km and 1.3 km deep.

7 THE LANDING SITE

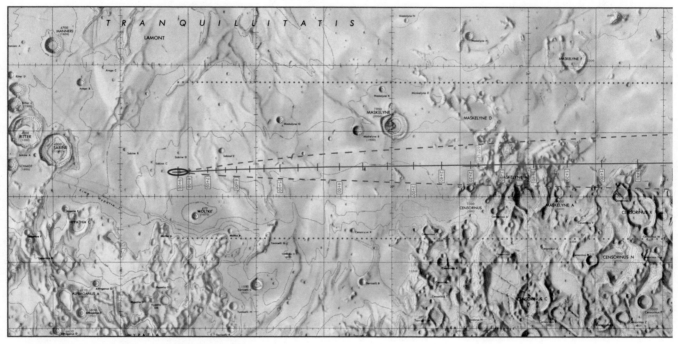

Lunar Descent monitoring chart - Left half.

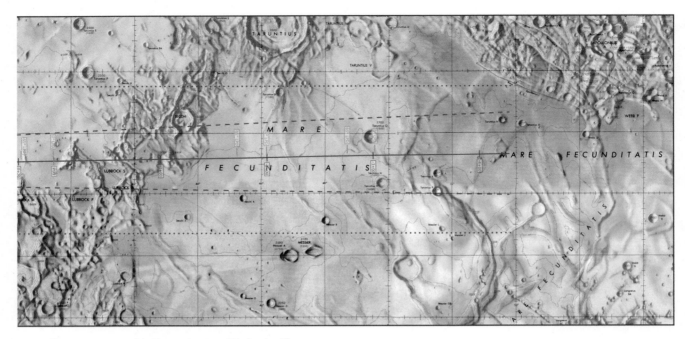

Lunar Descent monitoring chart - Right half.

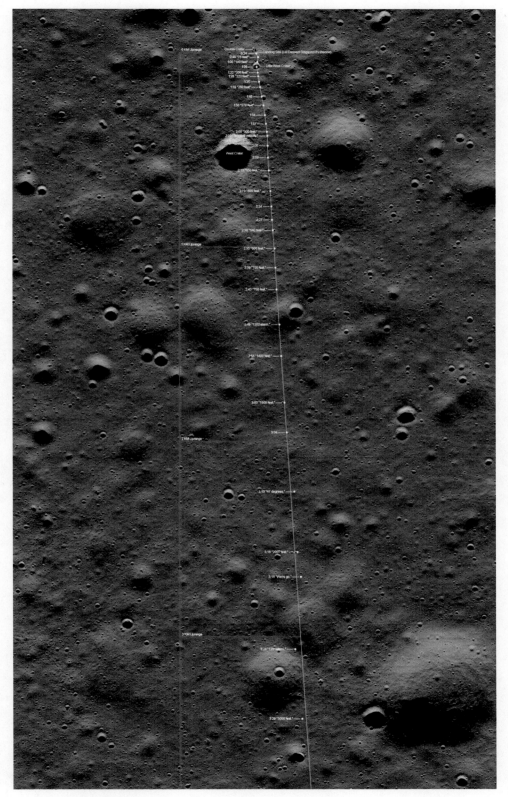

This map shows the ground track during the last 3 minutes 30 seconds of the descent. Each point is marked with the time remaining (mm:ss) until the landing. Many are labeled to indicate transmission from the crew.

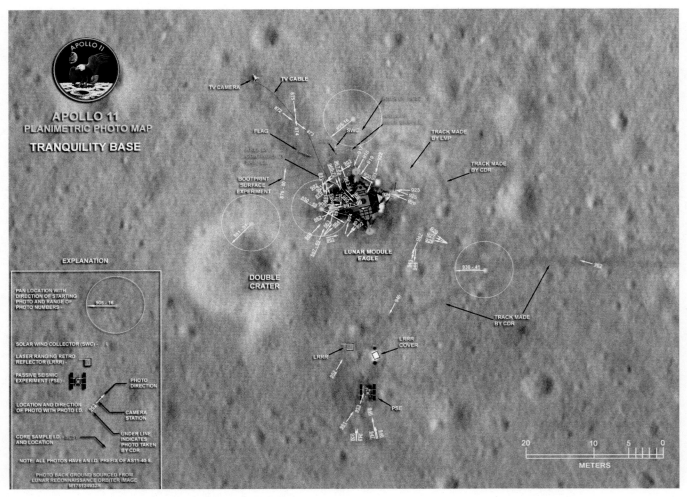

Lunar base showing crew activity locations.

(July 1969) --- A photographic illustration comparing the size of Apollo Landing Site 2 with that of the metropolitan Chicago, Illinois area. Site 2 is one of three Apollo 11 lunar landing sites. This will be the landing site if Apollo 11 is launched on July 16, 1969, as scheduled. Site 2 is located at 23 degrees 42 minutes 28 seconds east longitude and 0 degrees 42 minutes 50 seconds north latitude in southwestern Mare Tranquillitatis (Sea of Tranquility)

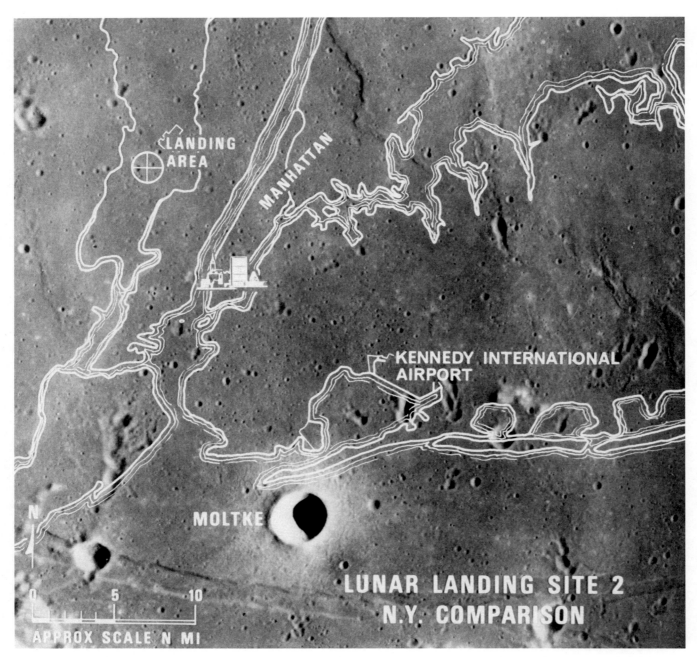

(July 1969) --- A photographic illustration comparing the size of Apollo Landing Site 2 with that of the metropolitan New York City area.

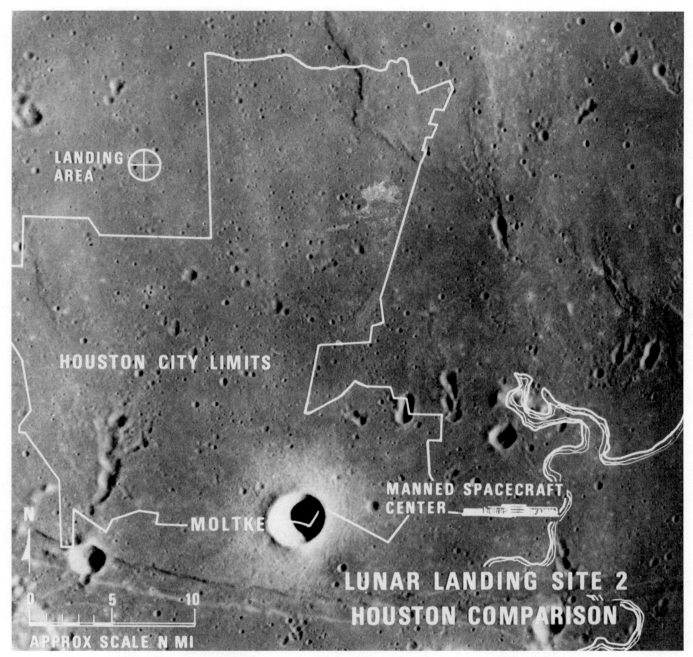

(July 1969) --- A photographic illustration comparing the size of Apollo Landing Site 2 with that of the metropolitan Houston, Texas area.

(20 July 1969) --- The approach to Apollo Landing Site 2 in southwestern Sea of Tranquility is seen in this photograph taken from the Apollo 11 Lunar Module (LM) in lunar orbit. When this picture was made, the LM was still docked to the Command and Service Modules (CSM). Site 2 is located just right of center at the edge of the darkness. The crater Maskelyne is the large one at the lower right. Hypatia Rille (U.S. 1) is at upper left, with the crater Moltke just to the right (north) of it. Sidewinder Rille and Diamondback Rille extend from left to right across the center of the picture. This view looks generally west.

The Apollo 11 Command and Service Modules (CSM) (tiny dot near quarter sized crater, center), with astronaut Michael Collins, command module pilot, aboard. The view overlooking the western Sea of Tranquility was photographed from the Lunar Module (LM). Astronauts Neil A. Armstrong, commander, and Edwin E. Aldrin Jr., lunar module pilot, manned the LM and made their historic lunar landing on July 20, 1969. Coordinates of the center of the terrain in the photograph are 18.5 degrees longitude and .5 degrees north latitude.

8 ON THE MOON – CREW ACTIVITIES

(20 July 1969) --- The deployment of the flag of the United States on the surface of the moon is captured on film during the first Apollo 11 lunar landing mission. Here, astronaut Neil A. Armstrong, commander, stands on the left at the flag's staff. Astronaut Edwin E. Aldrin Jr., lunar module pilot, is also pictured. The picture was taken from film exposed by the 16mm Data Acquisition Camera (DAC) which was mounted in the Lunar Module (LM). While astronauts Armstrong and Aldrin descended in the Lunar Module (LM) "Eagle" to explore the Sea of Tranquility region of the moon, astronaut Michael Collins, command module pilot, remained with the Command and Service Modules (CSM) "Columbia" in lunar orbit.

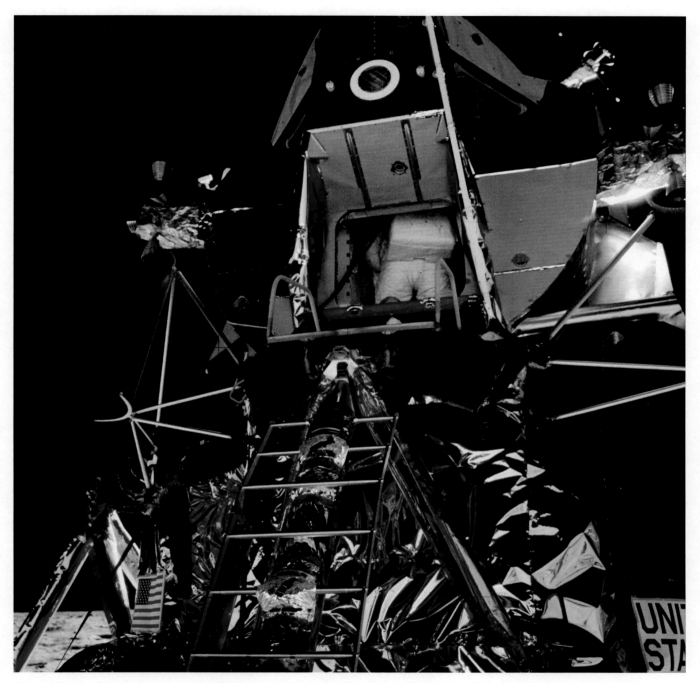

First photo of Buzz coming out through the hatch. The inward-opening hatch is on his left. Buzz is kneeling, probably with his hands on the midstep. We can see his heels, the lower portion of his PLSS and his left arm. Elsewhere in the image, both sets of thrusters are visible, along with Neil's window with the LPD grid etched on it, the straps of the Lunar Equipment Conveyor (LEC) coming out thru the hatch on the left, the upper portion of the ladder, the porch, and the plume deflector on the downward thruster on Buzz's side. The US flag that Neil and Buzz will deploy later is stowed in a long, thin canister attached to the underside of the lefthand rail of the ladder.

(20 July 1969) --- Astronaut Edwin E. Aldrin Jr., lunar module pilot, is photographed egressing the Lunar Module (LM) during the Apollo 11 extravehicular activity (EVA) on the moon. This photograph was taken by astronaut Neil A. Armstrong, commander, with a 70mm lunar surface camera. While astronauts Armstrong and Aldrin descended in the Lunar Module (LM) "Eagle" to explore the Sea of Tranquility region of the moon, astronaut Michael Collins, command module pilot, remained with the Command and Service Modules (CSM) "Columbia" in lunar orbit.

(20 July 1969) --- Astronaut Edwin E. Aldrin Jr., lunar module pilot, descends the steps of the Lunar Module (LM) ladder as he prepares to walk on the moon. He had just egressed the LM. This photograph was taken by astronaut Neil A. Armstrong, commander, with a 70mm lunar surface camera during the Apollo 11 extravehicular activity (EVA). While Armstrong and Aldrin descended in the LM "Eagle" to explore the moon, astronaut Michael Collins, command module pilot, remained with the Command and Service Modules (CSM) in lunar orbit.

(20 July 1969) --- Interior view of the Mission Operations Control Room (MOCR) in the Mission Control Center (MCC), Building 30, during the Apollo 11 lunar extravehicular activity (EVA). The television monitor shows astronauts Neil A. Armstrong and Edwin E. Aldrin Jr. on the surface of the moon.

(20 July 1969) --- Astronaut Edwin E. Aldrin Jr., lunar module pilot, is photographed during the Apollo 11 extravehicular activity (EVA) on the lunar surface. In the right background is the lunar module. On Aldrin's right is the Solar Wind Composition (SWC) experiment, already deployed. This photograph was taken by astronaut Neil A. Armstrong, commander, with a 70mm lunar surface camera.

Buzz attempting to drive the first of two on a core tubes into the surface. He was only able to get it in about 20 cm (8 inches). The Solar Wind Collector is just beyond the core tube and the TV camera is at the extreme left. Buzz's feedwater controls can be seen on the front, right hand corner of the bottom of his PLSS, as shown in a detail. Note the snap hook attached to the neckring tiedown strap hanging at the front of his suit. Note that areas where Neil and Buzz have disturbed and scattered soil are darker than undisturbed areas.

(20 July 1969) --- Astronaut Edwin E. Aldrin Jr., lunar module pilot, prepares to deploy the Early Apollo Scientific Experiments Package (EASEP) on the surface of the moon during the Apollo 11 extravehicular activity. Astronaut Neil A. Armstrong, commander, took this photograph with a 70mm lunar surface camera. In the foreground is the Apollo 11 35mm stereo close-up camera.

(20 July 1969) --- Astronaut Edwin E. Aldrin Jr., lunar module pilot, is photographed during the Apollo 11 extravehicular activity (EVA) on the moon. He has just deployed the Early Apollo Scientific Experiments Package (EASEP). This is a good view of the deployed equipment. In the foreground is the Passive Seismic Experiment Package (PSEP); beyond it is the Laser Ranging Retro-Reflector (LR-3); in the center background is the United States flag; in the left background is the black and white lunar surface television camera; in the far right background is the Lunar Module (LM). Astronaut Neil A. Armstrong, commander, took this picture with a 70mm lunar surface camera. While astronauts Armstrong and Aldrin descended in the Lunar Module (LM) "Eagle" to explore the Sea of Tranquility region of the moon, astronaut Michael Collins, command module pilot, remained with the Command and Service Modules (CSM) "Columbia" in lunar orbit.

Astronaut Buzz Aldrin, lunar module pilot of the first lunar landing mission, poses for a photograph beside the deployed United States flag during an Apollo 11 Extravehicular Activity (EVA) on the lunar surface. The Lunar Module (LM) is on the left, and the footprints of the astronauts are clearly visible in the soil of the Moon. Astronaut Neil A. Armstrong, commander, took this picture with a 70mm Hasselblad lunar surface camera. While astronauts Armstrong and Aldrin descended in the LM, the "Eagle", to explore the Sea of Tranquility region of the Moon, astronaut Michael Collins, command module pilot, remained with the Command and Service Modules (CSM) "Columbia" in lunar-orbit.

Buzz has placed the seismometer package on the surface and is using a built-in maneuvering handle to adjust the pointing and leveling. Note the dirt that he has pushed out of the way on the south side of the package in his attempt to get it level. Note, also, that the eastern rim of the double crater under Neil's LM window can be seen at the left edge of this photograph. The Gold camera is to the right of Buzz and the LRRR is to the left of him with the TV camera beyond.

(20 July 1969) --- Astronaut Edwin E. Aldrin Jr., lunar module pilot, walks on the surface of the moon near a leg of the Lunar Module during the Apollo 11 extravehicular activity (EVA). Astronaut Neil A. Armstrong, Apollo 11 commander, took this photograph with a 70mm lunar surface camera. The astronauts' bootprints are clearly visible in the foreground. While astronauts Armstrong and Aldrin descended in the Lunar Module (LM) "Eagle" to explore the Sea of Tranquility region of the moon, astronaut Michael Collins, command module pilot, remained with the Command and Service Modules (CSM) "Columbia" in lunar orbit.

(20 July 1969) --- Astronaut Edwin E. Aldrin Jr., lunar module pilot, walks on the surface of the moon near the leg of the Lunar Module (LM) "Eagle" during the Apollo 11 extravehicular activity (EVA). Astronaut Neil A. Armstrong, commander, took this photograph with a 70mm lunar surface camera. While astronauts Armstrong and Aldrin descended in the Lunar Module (LM) "Eagle" to explore the Sea of Tranquility region of the moon, astronaut Michael Collins, command module pilot, remained with the Command and Service Modules (CSM) "Columbia" in lunar orbit.

Buzz Aldrin moves toward a position to deploy two components of the Early Apollo Scientific Experiments Package (EASEP) on the surface of the moon during the Apollo 11 mission.

Buzz is standing just beyond the north strut. Note the distinctive dust smudges on Buzz's legs. The photo also shows the furrows in the bulk sample area and the area to the left of the footpad that shows unmistakable signs of sweeping by the descent engine exhaust.

Buzz is preparing to remove the passive seismometer from the lefthand compartment in the SEQ bay. The LRRR is in the righthand compartment. The bay is between the east and south struts and has two doors: a vertically-hinged door at Buzz's left and a horizontally-hinged door which can be seen above the right side of the bay. Buzz pulled on a pulley-mounted tape to raise the latter door.

9 ON THE MOON – LUNAR PHOTOS

First EVA picture. Neil's first frame in a pan taken west of the ladder. Jettison bag under the Descent Stage, south footpad, bent probe, strut supports. The view is more or less up-Sun, so we are seeing the shadowed faces of boulders. 20 July 1969.

Buzz still has the Hasselblad camera and is taking photographs while he does an inspection of the LM. This is a close-up of the north footpad, showing the buried probe.

Buzz took this picture of the surface beneath the LM from near the minus-Y (south) strut. The engine bell is at the upper left. The probe on the south footpad is at right center and we can see how that probe was dragged from the initial contact point. The jettison bag is in the foreground, with two anonymous pieces of trash next to it. They may be pieces of padding from the Sample Return Container (SRC), also known as the rock box, which Neil opened shortly after deploying the TV.

(20 July 1969) --- A close-up view of an astronaut's bootprint in the lunar soil, photographed with a 70mm lunar surface camera during the Apollo 11 extravehicular activity (EVA) on the moon. While astronauts Neil A. Armstrong, commander, and Edwin E. Aldrin Jr., lunar module pilot, descended in the Lunar Module (LM) "Eagle" to explore the Sea of Tranquility region of the moon, astronaut Michael Collins, command module pilot, remained with the Command and Service Modules (CSM) "Columbia" in lunar orbit.

(20 July 1969) --- A close-up view of an astronaut's boot and bootprint in the lunar soil, photographed with a 70mm lunar surface camera during the Apollo 11 lunar surface extravehicular activity (EVA). While astronauts Neil A. Armstrong, commander, and Edwin A. Aldrin Jr., lunar module pilot, descended in the Lunar Module (LM) "Eagle" to explore the Sea of Tranquility region of the moon, astronaut Michael Collins, command module pilot, remained with the Command and Service Modules (CSM)" Columbia" in lunar orbit.

View of lunar surface after EVA completion with the flag and the TV camera.

Lunar horizon from Tranquility Base, the Lunar Module (LM) landing site. Unites States flag and LM thruster shadow visible on lunar surface. Image taken from inside the LM during the Apollo 11 Mission.

(20 July 1969) --- The flag of the United States, deployed on the surface of the moon, dominates this photograph taken from inside the Lunar Module (LM). The footprints of astronauts Neil A. Armstrong and Edwin E. Aldrin Jr. stand out very clearly. In the far background is the deployed black and white lunar surface television camera which televised the Apollo 11 lunar surface extravehicular activity (EVA). While astronauts Armstrong, commander, and Aldrin, lunar module pilot, descended in the Lunar Module (LM) "Eagle" to explore the Sea of Tranquility region of the moon, astronaut Michael Collins, command module pilot, remained with the Command and Service Modules (CSM) "Columbia" in lunar orbit.

(20 July 1969) --- This photograph shows in fine detail the impressions in the lunar soil made by astronauts Neil A. Armstrong and Edwin E. Aldrin Jr. during their lunar surface extravehicular activity (EVA). While astronauts Armstrong, commander, and Aldrin, lunar module pilot, descended in the Lunar Module (LM) "Eagle" to explore the Sea of Tranquility region of the moon, astronaut Michael Collins, command module pilot, remained with the Command and Service Modules (CSM) "Columbia" in lunar orbit.

(20 July 1969) --- This crater which was located near the point the Apollo 11 Lunar Module (LM) touched down on the moon was photographed by the Apollo 11 astronauts during their lunar surface extravehicular activity (EVA). Dark shadows obscure much of the crater wall in the background. Michael Collins, command module pilot, remained with the Command and Service Modules (CSM) in lunar orbit while Neil A. Armstrong, commander, and Edwin E. Aldrin Jr., lunar module pilot, explored the moon. The object in the foreground is the Apollo 11 35mm stereo close-up camera.

View of lunar surface after EVA completion. The younger member of the double crater is at the lower right and the older member is at the lower left.

(20 July 1969) --- This 70mm handheld camera's image on the Sea of Tranquility's lunar surface is the first of a multi-framed panorama photographed from a point some 30 or 40 feet west of the plus-Z (west) footpad of the Lunar Module "Eagle." The view is looking toward the southwest showing part of the horizon crater rim that was pointed out as being visible from the Eagle's window.

View towards the South. The LRRR (18 meters from the minus-Y footpad) is to the right of the vertical RCS thruster, while the PSEP antenna (24 meters from the minus-Y footpad) is partly visible above the top of the thruster.

10 STUNNING EARTH VIEWS

(16-24 July 1969) --- This view from the Apollo 11 spacecraft shows Earth rising above the moon's horizon. The lunar terrain pictured is in the area of Smyth's Sea on the nearside. Coordinates of the center of the terrain are 86 degrees east longitude and 3 degrees north latitude.

(July 1969) --- Near vertical view of Mexico, and a portion of the southwest United States, as photographed from the Apollo 11 spacecraft during its trans-Earth journey homeward. Onboard Apollo 11 were astronauts Neil A. Armstrong, Michael Collins and Edwin E. Aldrin Jr.

(16 July 1969) --- This view of Earth showing clouds over its surface was photographed from the Apollo 11 spacecraft during its translunar journey toward the moon. The spacecraft was already about 10,000 nautical miles from Earth when this picture was taken. Portions of the land mass of North America and Central America can be seen. Aboard Apollo 11 were astronauts Neil A. Armstrong, Michael Collins and Edwin E. Aldrin Jr.

(16-24 July 1969) --- This view of Earth rising over the moon's horizon was taken from the Apollo spacecraft. The lunar terrain pictured is in the area of Smyth's Sea on the nearside. Coordinates of the center of the terrain are 85 degrees east longitude and 3 degrees north latitude. While astronaut Neil A. Armstrong, commander; and Edwin E. Aldrin Jr., lunar module pilot, descended in the Lunar Module (LM) "Eagle" to explore the Sea of Tranquility region of the moon, astronaut Michael Collins remained with the Command and Service Modules (CSM) "Columbia" in lunar orbit.

Earthrise. Bright crater in foreground is Al-Khwarizmi K. Mare Smythii and Mare Marginis on horizon.

View of the Lunar Module (LM) ascent stage. The Earth is visible above the LM. Image taken at Tranquility Base during the Apollo 11 Mission. Original film magazine was labeled S. Film Type: Ektachrome EF SO168 color film on a 2.7-mil Estar polyester base taken with a 60mm lens. Sun angle is Medium. Tilt direction is Southwest (SW).

(16-24 July 1969) --- One-third of the Earth's sphere illuminated, Earth's terminator, sunglint, a portion of east Africa, as photographed from the Apollo 11 spacecraft during its first lunar landing mission. While astronauts Neil A. Armstrong, commander, and Edwin E. Aldrin Jr., lunar module pilot, descended in the Lunar Module (LM) "Eagle" to explore the Sea of Tranquility region of the moon, astronaut Michael Collins, command module pilot, remained with the Command and Service Modules (CSM) "Columbia" in lunar orbit.

11 THE TRIP BACK AND HOME

On July 21, 1969, only days after walking on the Moon's surface, Neil Armstrong and Buzz Aldrin leave lunar orbit and begin the journey back to the space ship Columbia and its return to Earth. As they leave the Moon's orbit, a look back gives them a new perspective of where they were and where man's future lies. This was their final sight of the moon before they began docking

(21 July 1969) --- This outstanding view of the whole full moon was photographed from the Apollo 11 spacecraft during its trans-Earth journey homeward. When this picture was taken, the spacecraft was already 10,000 nautical miles away. Onboard Apollo 11 were astronauts Neil A. Armstrong, commander; Michael Collins, command module pilot; and Edwin E. Aldrin Jr., lunar module pilot. While astronauts Armstrong and Aldrin descended in the Lunar Module (LM) "Eagle" to explore the moon, astronaut Collins remained with the Command and Service Modules (CSM) "Columbia" in lunar orbit.

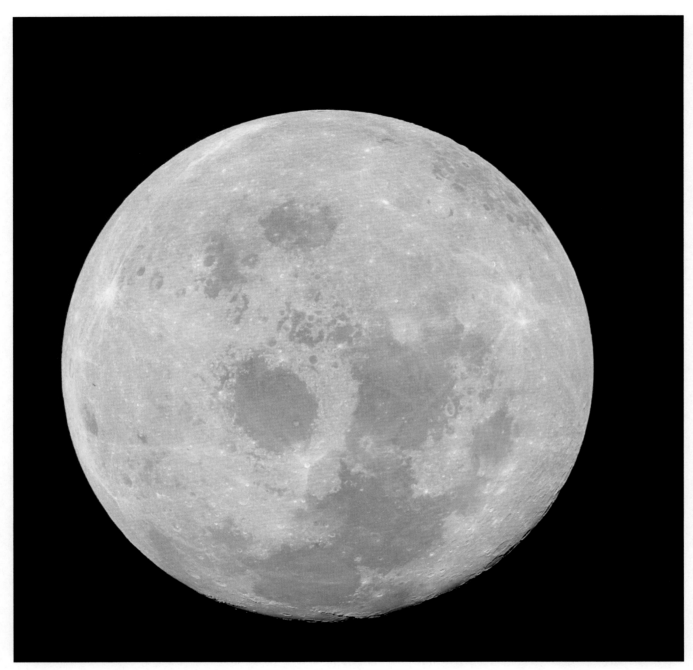

Taken with a 250-mm lens. Mare Crisium left of centre .

(24 May 1969) --- The third member of the prime crew of the Apollo 11 lunar landing mission egresses Apollo Boilerplate 1102 during water egress training in the Gulf of Mexico. The other two crewmen are in raft. Taking part in the training were astronauts Neil A. Armstrong, commander; Michael Collins, command module pilot; and Edwin E. Aldrin Jr., lunar module pilot. The three crewmen practiced donning and wearing biological isolation garments (B.I.G.) as a part of the exercise. The Manned Spacecraft Center (MSC) swimmer standing up, who assisted in the training, is also wearing a B.I.G.

Apollo 11 crew in isolation suits after splashdown. 24 July 1969.

(24 July 1969) --- The three Apollo 11 crew men await pickup by a helicopter from the USS Hornet, prime recovery ship for the historic Apollo 11 lunar landing mission. The fourth man in the life raft is a United States Navy underwater demolition team swimmer. All four men are wearing biological isolation garments. Apollo 11, with astronauts Neil A. Armstrong, commander; Michael Collins, command module pilot; and Edwin E. Aldrin Jr., lunar module pilot, onboard, splashed down at 11:49 a.m. (CDT), July 24, 1969, about 812 nautical miles southwest of Hawaii and only 12 nautical miles from the USS Hornet. While astronauts Armstrong and Aldrin descended in the Lunar Module (LM) "Eagle" to explore the Sea of Tranquility region of the moon, astronaut Collins remained with the Command and Service Modules (CSM) "Columbia" in lunar orbit.

The Apollo 11 Command Module (CM) is photographed as it is hoisted aboard the USS Hornet, prime recovery vessel for the historic Apollo 11 lunar landing mission. The splashdown took place at 11:49 a.m. (CDT), July 24, 1969, about 812 nautical miles southwest of Hawaii, only 12 nautical miles from the USS Hornet.

(24 July 1969) --- The Apollo 11 crewmen, wearing biological isolation garments, arrive aboard the USS Hornet during recovery operations in the central Pacific. They are walking toward the Mobile Quarantine Facility (MQF), in which they will be confined until they arrive at the Manned Spacecraft Center's (MSC), Lunar Receiving Laboratory (LRL). Apollo 11, with astronauts Neil A. Armstrong, commander; Michael Collins, command module pilot; and Edwin E. Aldrin Jr., lunar module pilot, onboard, splashed down at 11:49 a.m. (CDT), July 24, 1969, about 812 nautical miles southwest of Hawaii and only 12 nautical miles from the USS Hornet to conclude their historic lunar landing mission.

Offloading of the Mobile Quarantine Facility from the USS Hornet, to be sent to Hickam AFB, Hawaii. 26 July 1969.

Within the White Room atop the gantry on Launch Complex 39 Pad A, the Apollo 11 astronauts egress from the Apollo spacecraft after participation in the Countdown Demonstration Test. In the foreground of the photograph is Astronaut Buzz Aldrin. Pad leader Guenter Wendt talks with Neil Armstrong.

(27 July 1969) --- The Apollo 11 crewmen, still under a 21-day quarantine, are greeted by their wives. They arrived at Ellington Air Force Base very early Sunday after a flight aboard a U.S. Air Force C-141 transport from Hawaii. Looking through the window of a Mobile Quarantine Facility (MQF) are (left to right) astronauts Neil A. Armstrong, Edwin E. Aldrin Jr., and Michael Collins. The wives are (left to right) Mrs. Pat Collins, Mrs. Jan Armstrong, and Mrs. Joan Aldrin. The crew of the historic Apollo 11 lunar landing mission remained in the MQF until they arrived to the Crew Reception Area of the Lunar Receiving Laboratory at the Manned Spacecraft Center (MSC).

(30 July 1969) --- The crewmen of the historic Apollo 11 lunar landing mission stand in the serving line as they prepare to dine in the Crew Reception Area of the Lunar Receiving Laboratory, Building 37, Manned Spacecraft Center. Left to right, are astronauts Edwin E. Aldrin Jr., Michael Collins, and Neil A. Armstrong. They are continuing their postflight debriefings. The three astronauts will be released from quarantine on Aug. 11, 1969.

(30 July 1969) --- The crewmen of the historic Apollo 11 lunar landing mission are seen dining in the Crew Reception Area of the Lunar Receiving Laboratory, Building 37, Manned Spacecraft Center. Left to right, are astronauts Edwin E. Aldrin Jr., Michael Collins, and Neil A. Armstrong. They are continuing their postflight debriefings. The astronauts will be released from quarantine on Aug. 11, 1969.

The first Apollo 11 sample return container, containing lunar surface material, arrives at Ellington Air Force Base by air from the Pacific recovery area. Happily posing for photographs with the rock box are (left to right) George M. Low, Manager, Apollo Spacecraft Program, Manned Spacecraft Center (MSC); U.S. Air Force Lt. Gen. Samuel C. Phillips, Apollo Program Director, Office of Manned Space Flight, NASA HQ.; George S. Trimble, MSC Deputy Director (almost obscured); Eugene G. Edmonds, MSC Photographic Technology Laboratory; Richard S. Johnston, M.D. (in back), Special Assistant to the MSC Director; Dr. Thomas O. Paine, NASA Administrator; and Dr. Robert R. Gilruth, MSC Director.

This is the second rock box Neil filled on the lunar surface. It is the Documented Sample Apollo Lunar Sample Retrun Container and contains approximately 20 grab samples weighing a total of 5.5 kilograms. Neil collected these in about 3 1/2 minutes before starting closeout activities. As he used the tongs to collect a representative sampling of rocks, he put them in a 'weigh bag' made of teflon film. Once he was done, he put the entire weigh bag in the rockbox. In the photo, we see that the weigh bag has been torn open to reveal the rocks. Neil also packed the two core tubes in this box and these can be seen at the upper left. The gloved right hand of the vacuum-chamber operator is at the lower right. 26 July 1969.

(24 July 1969) --- Overall view of the Mission Operations Control Room (MOCR) in the Mission Control Center (MCC), Building 30, Manned Spacecraft Center (MSC), showing the flight controllers celebrating the successful conclusion of the Apollo 11 lunar landing mission.

(24 July 1969) --- Overall view of the Mission Operations Control Room (MOCR) in the Mission Control Center (MCC), Building 30, Manned Spacecraft Center (MSC), showing the flight controllers celebrating the successful conclusion of the Apollo 11 lunar landing mission.

Traditional post-flight cake cutting ceremony was altered because the Apollo 11 astronauts were restricted to the Mobile Quarantine Facility. Photo filed 24 July 1969.

(13 Aug. 1969) --- New York City welcomes Apollo 11 crewmen in a showering of ticker tape down Broadway and Park Avenue in a parade termed as the largest in the city's history. Pictured in the lead car, from the right, are astronauts Neil A. Armstrong, commander; Michael Collins, command module pilot; and Edwin E. Aldrin Jr., lunar module pilot. The three astronauts teamed for the first manned lunar landing, on July 20, 1969

(13 Aug. 1969) --- New York City welcomes Apollo 11 crewmen in a showering of ticker tape down Broadway and Park Avenue in a parade termed as the largest in the city's history. Pictured in the lead car, from the right, are astronauts Neil A. Armstrong, commander; Michael Collins, command module pilot; and Edwin E. Aldrin Jr., lunar module pilot. The three astronauts teamed for the first manned lunar landing, on July 20, 1969.

12 ERRATA

(July 1969) --- TRW Incorporated's artist concept depicting the Apollo 11 Lunar Module (LM) descending to the surface of the moon. Inside the LM will be astronauts Neil A. Armstrong, commander, and Edwin E. Aldrin Jr., lunar module pilot. Astronaut Michael Collins, command module pilot, will remain with the Command and Service Modules (CSM) in lunar orbit. TRW's LM descent engine will brake Apollo 11's descent to the lunar surface. The throttle-able rocket engine will be fired continuously the last 10 miles of the journey to the moon, slowing the LM to a speed of two miles per hour at touchdown. TRW Incorporated designed and built the unique engine at Redondo Beach, California under subcontract to the Grumman Aircraft Engineering Corporation, Bethpage, New York, the LM prime contractor.

(July 1969) --- Rocketdyne's artist concept depicting the firing of the ascent engine as the Apollo 11 Lunar Module (LM) ascent stage is launched from the surface of the moon. The descent stage serves as a launch base and remains on the lunar surface. Inside the LM are astronauts Neil A. Armstrong, commander; and Edwin E. Aldrin Jr., lunar module pilot. Astronaut Michael Collins, command module pilot, remains with the Command and Service Modules (CSM) in lunar orbit while Armstrong and Aldrin explore the moon. The LM ascent stage from the lunar surface and place it in proper trajectory for rendezvous with the CSM. Rocketdyne, a division of North American Rockwell Corporation, is the subcontractor for the LM ascent engine. Grumman Aircraft Engineering Corporation, Bethpage, New York, is the LM prime contractor.

Apollo 11 patch.

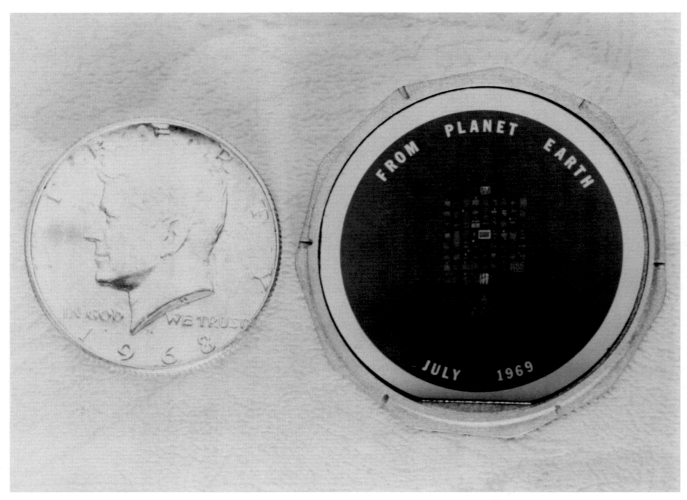

(July 1969) --- Close-up view of the one and one-half inch silicon disk which will be left on the moon by the Apollo 11 astronauts. The disk bears messages of goodwill from heads of state of many nations. The process used to make this wafer is the same as that used to manufacture integrated circuits for electronic equipment. It involves making tiny photographic images and depositing metal on the images. The Kennedy half-dollar illustrates the relative size of the memorial disk.

(July 1969) --- Close-up view of the one and one-half inch silicon disk which will be left on the moon by the Apollo 11 astronauts. The disk bears messages of goodwill from heads of state of many nations. The process used to make this wafer is the same as that used to manufacture integrated circuits for electronic equipment. It involves making tiny photographic images and depositing metal on the images. The Kennedy half-dollar illustrates the relative size of the memorial disk.

(July 1969) --- Close-up view of the plaque which the Apollo 11 astronauts will leave behind on the moon in commemoration of the historic event. The plaque is made of stainless steel measuring nine by seven and five-eights inches, and one-sixteenth inch thick. The plaque will be attached to the ladder on the landing gear strut on the descent stage of the Apollo 11 Lunar Module (LM). Covering the plaque during flight will be a thin sheet of stainless steel which will be removed on the lunar surface.

HERE MEN FROM THE PLANET EARTH
FIRST SET FOOT UPON THE MOON
JULY 1969, A. D.
WE CAME IN PEACE FOR ALL MANKIND

NEIL A. ARMSTRONG
ASTRONAUT

MICHAEL COLLINS
ASTRONAUT

EDWIN E. ALDRIN, JR.
ASTRONAUT

RICHARD NIXON
PRESIDENT, UNITED STATES OF AMERICA

(July 1969) --- This is a replica of the plaque which the Apollo 11 astronauts will leave behind on the moon in commemoration of the historic event. The plaque is made of stainless steel, measuring nine by seven and five-eighths inches, and one-sixteenth inch thick. The plaque will be attached to the ladder on the landing gear strut on the descent stage of the Apollo 11 Lunar Module (LM). Covering the plaque during the flight will be a thin sheet of stainless steel which will be removed on the lunar surface.

ABOUT THE AUTHOR

Steven Chabotte is an author and entrepreneur. He enjoys working with public domain materials to build exciting new products to share the joys of the past with others and this book is one example of that – sharing the most exciting mission to the moon in pictures.

Made in the USA
San Bernardino, CA
19 July 2019